Tell us what you see!

The Bed Sheet Parachute
Tangles and Rhymes

Favorite poems from
Thinking Upside Down
and
Stars to Chase
written and illustrated by
Byron von Rosenberg

The Bed Sheet Parachute
Copyright © 2017 Byron von Rosenberg
All rights reserved

Cover design by Byron von Rosenberg
Interior design by Sharon von Rosenberg
Favorite poems from his books ***Thinking Upside Down*** and ***Stars to Chase***

Published by
Red Mountain Creations
P. O. Box 172
High Ridge, MO 63049
www.idontwanttokissallama.com
redmountain@swbell.net

Publisher's Cataloging-in-Publication Data

von Rosenberg, Byron

The Bed Sheet Parachute : Poetry Juvenile / Byron von Rosenberg.—
1st ed. – High Ridge, MO : Red Mountain Creations, 2017

p. ; cm.

ISBN   978-0-9910804-3-4

    1.   Inspiration – Poetry. 2.Juvenille poetry. I. Title.

All rights reserved. No part of this book may be reproduced, stored in a retrieval system or transmitted in any form or by any means – electronic, mechanical, photocopying, recording or otherwise – without prior permission in writing from the copyright holder except as provided by USA copyright law.

Printed in the United States of America by Bang Printing, Brainerd, MN.

Dedicated to
Dale von Rosenberg
Husband, Father and Grandfather

Who gave us free balloons
and let us play in puddles!

PUDDLES

It takes a lot of effort
To splash the mud all out
But then I get to take it home.
Can't wait to hear Mom shout!
The poet that I am today
Sits around and muddles
But the little boy inside of me
Would rather play in puddles.

An alphabetical list of poems begins on page 158.
You may find "Free Balloons" on page 155.

THE BED SHEET PARACHUTE

There was not a tree he couldn't climb
For miles and miles around
And it's said that little Leon
Never liked it on the ground.
One day his friends came calling
And hollered up the tree,
"Why don't you ride this bed sheet down
And tell us what you see?
You'd better do it, Leon!
There ain't no turning back!"
Such taunts can lead to pain
When it's common sense you lack.
Leon grabbed the corners
And leapt off of the limb.
If the bed sheet hadn't tangled,
There'd be nothing left of him.

When his father found him later
He was still quite badly stuck
And told him he should say his fate
Was, "Stupidity! Not bad luck."
So no matter what the pressure is
To succumb to such a dare
Remember the bed sheet parachute
And my advice,

"BEWARE!"

This is a true story told to me by an elderly gentleman in Branson, MO.
He grew up in Oklahoma.

"Thinking Upside Down" is what I thought when I tried to get up too fast from a nap and felt dizzy. About half of the poems in this book are from my book of the same name. The poem continues through page 9.

THINKING UPSIDE DOWN

I had a dream this morning
And I think I was a bat
'Cause I was hanging upside down!
How can they think like that?
"Keep your feet off of the ceiling!"
That's what my mother said.
"If you put your feet up
Your blood all rushes to your head!"

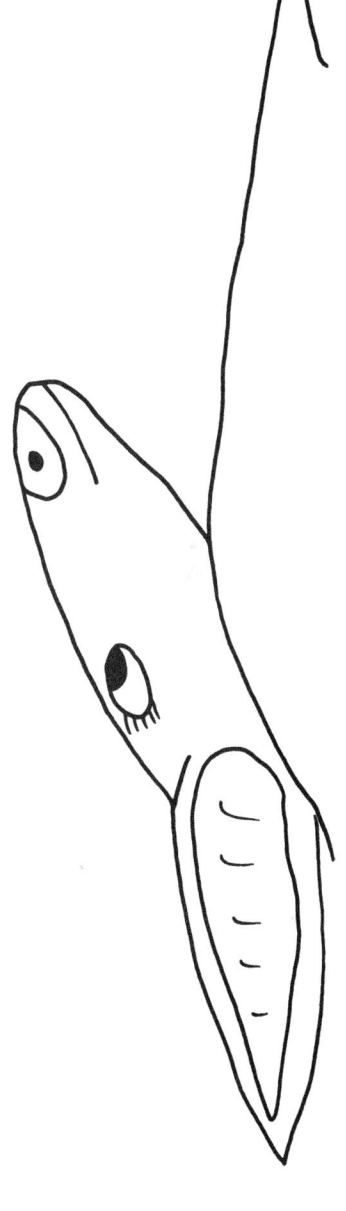

So how is it that mother bats
Have this lesson switched about?
For when you think upside down
It creates odd looks and doubt!
We say that bats are batty,

Their flight so u n p r e d i c t a b l e.
It's names like that we people use

To make others' thoughts **CON**strictable.

Yet a bat can catch ten thousand bugs
And I can't swat a fly,
And if I'm thinking for myself
I can figure out just why.

Yes, anyone who's different
Is called a freak or clown.
But sometimes great advancements come
From thinking upside down!

THE OTTER OUGHTER

The otter oughter work!
It plays just way too much.
It oughter spend its time
Doing chores and such.
The otter oughter wipe that smile
Right off its silly face,
Get with all the other rats
And live life like a race!
The otter oughter schedule
And organize its time.
Such idleness is sinful!
Why, it's almost a crime!
The otter oughter get a job,
Keep its money in a bank.
When it makes these changes
It will have me to thank!
Odd the otter knows
The best in life is free.
The otter oughter teach
That lesson now to me!

My wife and daughter saw an otter by the side of a busy road in Branson. I thought it ought to get out of the way.

"Arnot and Artu" relates to my childhood rivalry with my sister, how we resolved it and the name of a road in the Texas Panhandle.

ARNOT AND ARTU, THE LLAMAS FROM FRANCE

Arnot and Artu were llamas from France
Who couldn't agree on their cans and their can'ts.
Arnot would say "No" to his sister Artu
Who ended up taking the opposite view.
The subject in question never did matter
And their arguments ended in spit and in splatter
Until on the day Arnot realized
If he'd agree with his sister they'd both be surprised.
Artu was amazed and responded in kind
And if you'd do the same I think that you'd find
That the people who love you are worth taking that chance
Like Arnot and Artu, the llamas from France.

SUPER-FROG

He could leap over the dog house.
It took just a single bound!
He hopped faster than a rabbit
And he sure could cover ground.
He could snap his tongue and catch a bug
Twenty feet away
And any kid who picked him up
Was repelled by his awesome spray.
He was the biggest strongest frog
The planet's ever seen.
His amphibious friends all envied him.
(That's why they're all still green.)
He didn't have a thing to prove
For his fame was widely known
But he wanted to stop a train like Superman
To show how strong he'd grown.
He hopped down to the station
To catch the nine o'clock.
He waited across the street
To show off for his webbed-foot flock.
When the nine o'clock came rolling in
He jumped high across the road
But not high enough to miss my car…

And I squashed him like a toad!

Super-Frog, oh, Super-Frog!
Why did it have to end like that?
In his epic last performance
Super-Frog seemed a little flat!

Super-Frog is a cartoon. He always survives disaster.

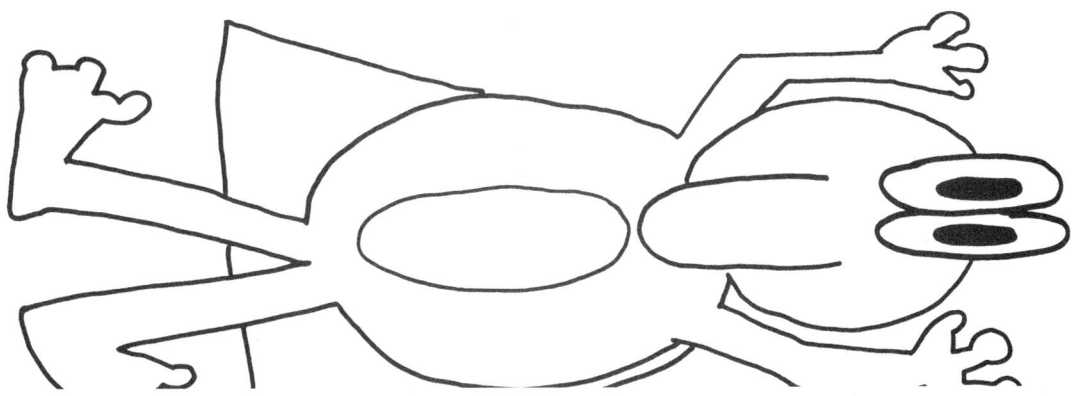

"The Ballad of Peanut Butter Pete" commemorates the fanaticism of a dear friend (who by request shall remain anonymous) for that yummy food. The poem continues through page 16.

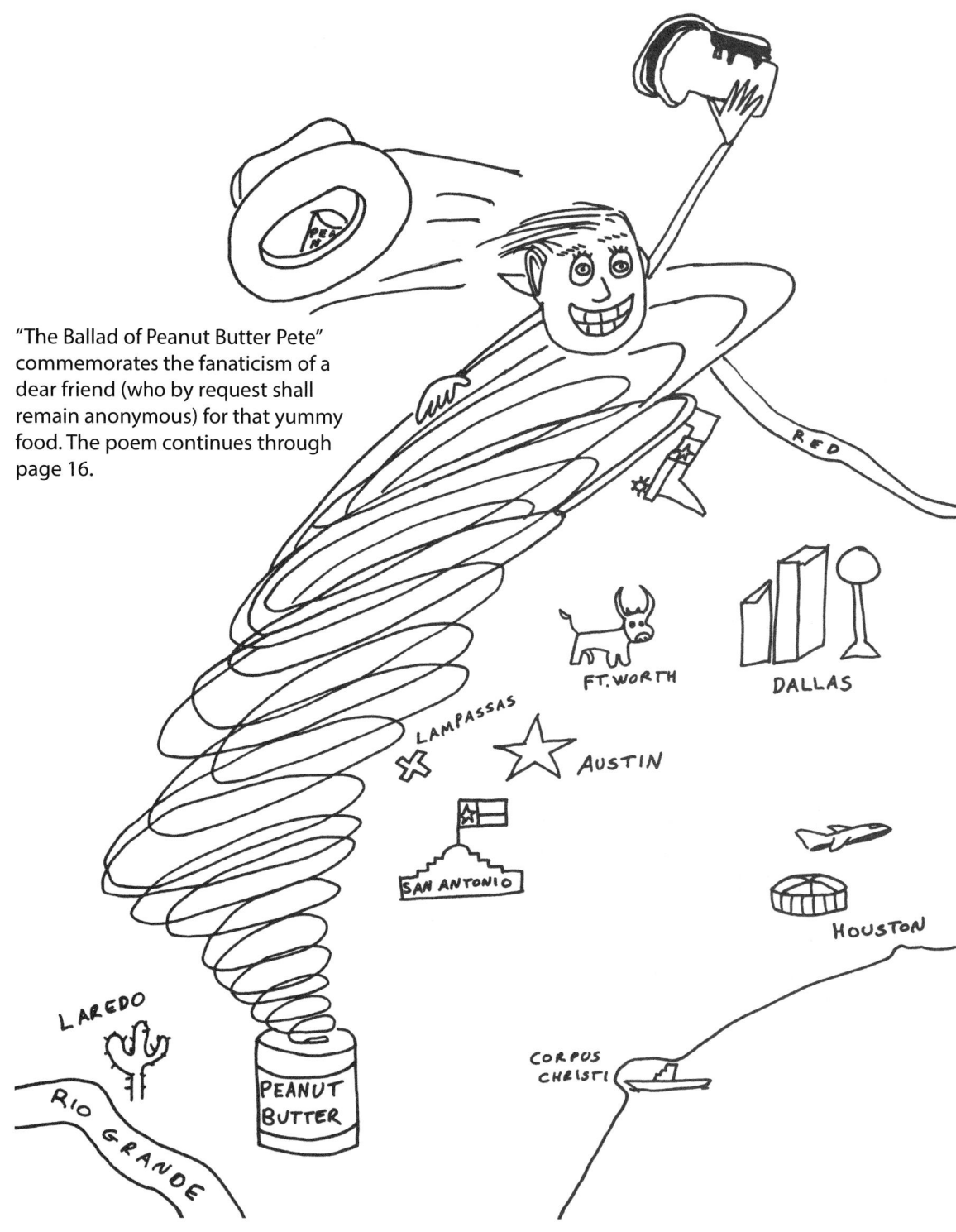

THE BALLAD OF PEANUT BUTTER PETE

He roped a twister like Pecos Bill and rode it in a test of will
Across the entire Lone Star state until the great winds did abate.
They cheered him down in Mexico, "Viva, viva! What a show!
From the Red to the Rio Grande! How, Pete, how?" He held out his hand.
"PBJ," he said with a smile, "helps me hold on quite a while.
On my hand or in my tummy, that's the best, for it's quite yummy,
Straight out of a gallon jar or from a shot glass at the bar!
My momma put it in my soup. It tasted good and cured the croup.
It's the only thing I'll ever eat. Hi! I'm Peanut Butter Pete!"
Across the west his legend grew and he owed it all to that sticky goo.
He ran for sheriff on a bet with a winning phrase they can't forget:
"He'll stick it out through thin and thick. His aim is sure and his draw is quick!
It's peanut butter, not molasses. Vote for Pete here in Lampassas!"
He won two hundred votes to twenty and brought in PBJ aplenty.

He kept a stash 'most everywhere – in his desk, beside his chair,
'Neath the saddle of his horse (just to hold it on, of course).
Never once did he admit, "It's PB's fault my pants don't fit!"
It filled the holster of his gun and in a duel he was undone
For his pistol stuck and wouldn't fire. He was bleedin' bad, his chances dire.
"Doc," he said, "give it to me straight." "You're gonna die, Pete, it's much too late."
"Not too late!" they heard him utter. "Bring me all my peanut butter!"
He ate and ate, then they heard him roar, "I'm feeling better! Bring me more!"
They brought it out in gallons and tubs and lathered him with massages and rubs
And then the tearful eyes were dry as they heard the doctor's cheerful cry.
"Glory be! God rest my soul! The PBJ's filled up the hole!"
He wobbled slowly to his feet and ambled gamely down the street.
He lived to see another day, thanks in full to PBJ.
Now here's the jelly, here's the bread. Lay on thick that glorious spread!
And now pretend you're PB Pete. It's lunchtime, kid. Sit down and eat!

PROPHET THE LLAMA

Prophet the Llama was split half and half.
It turned people's heads and made most of them laugh.
He always stood rigid. He never did sway
And no one could ever find one hair of gray.
He was black on one side and white on the other,
A fact that perturbed his father and mother
For he wasn't like them to go along with the herd.
If he saw it that way, he'd call it absurd.
He didn't have many friends for being so curt
For llamas, like people, get their feelings hurt.

But when they had to decide which way to go
The llamas all knew that Prophet would know.
He'd tell them the truth (he never did fail)
And point right or left with his two-colored tail.
I've known people like Prophet who never blink.
They look ordinary but, in truth, are distinct.
For truth is a commodity sacred and rare
That shows in your heart much more than your hair.
In the face of a lie, can you say what is true?
Then you'll stand out like Prophet and we'll all look to you.

"Prophet the Llama" is really a black and white horse that we see in a pasture near Bourbon, Missouri.

LEAP FROM YOUR DREAMS

It seems like I am stuck
In my dreams 'most all the time.
I just can't get out.
It's too hard a climb.
This morning I decided
I would finally escape
And swing out of my dreams
On the backside of an ape!
It swung high and low
And touched 'most every tree,
But it had no real direction
and was of no help to me.
I got a ride upon a hippo.
Now that was quite a blunder!
I couldn't get a grip
And kept on sliding under!
And then it got much worse.
It swam into the lake!
Whatever you may do,
Please don't make my mistake.

Next I tried an antelope.
Boy, do they run fast!
But it would never stop!
It kept on going past.
All the places I would see
Were gone in just a blink.
I'd like to slow it down a bit
And enjoy my life, I think!

Now the next thing that I did
Might appeal somewhat to you.
I got inside the pouch
Of a giant kangaroo!
But it was way to bumpy
With the starting and the stopping.
To get out of my dreams
Will take much more than hopping.

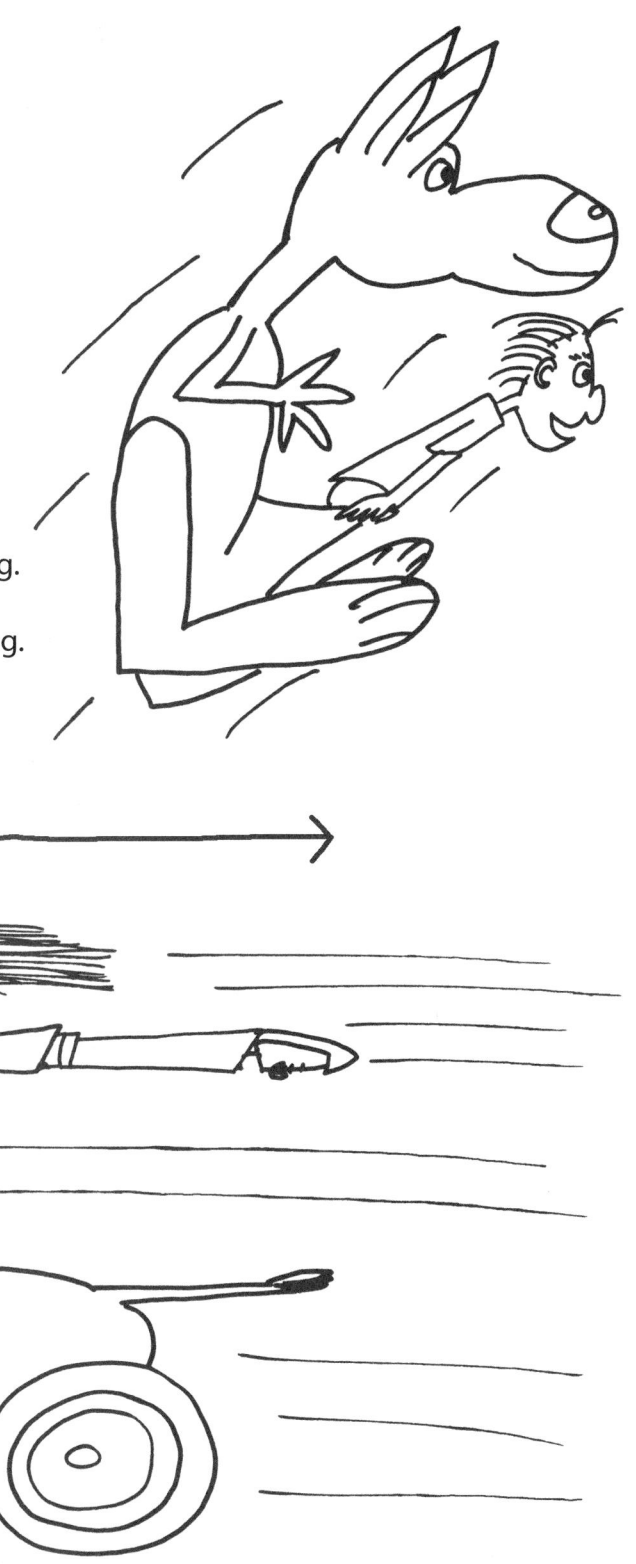

And in sadness I looked down.
Hey! There are two good feet!
Maybe they can jump
And wouldn't that be neat!
They're not built as are an ape's
To grab onto a vine.
They're not giant like a hippo's
But the good thing is – they're mine!
They can't keep up with an antelope
Or hop like that big 'roo,
But to leap out of my dreams
Just this pair alone will do.
So I thanked all of the animals
For the kindness they had shown
But I'll leap out of my dreams
With these two feet of my own!
Yes, now you know the secret-
To seek out your own way! -
So leap out of your dreams
And into this great day!

Written at my mother's house in Texas before a Kiwanis club meeting I had to get up for.

INVASION OF THE WOODPECKERS

I listened to the woodpecker
As it knocked upon the tree.
Knowing that it ate parasites
Was comforting to me.
I was delighted when two of them
Flew over from next door
But did not know what to do
When I saw a hundred more.
The sky was dark with woodpeckers.
The trees were shaking with their blows!
By spring these ravaged trees would die
For with such damage nothing grows.
The woodpeckers kept on pecking
After all the bugs and bark were gone.
They kept on sinking holes all night
And there were more of them by dawn!
The invasion of the woodpeckers
Is an awesome, dreadful sight
And the next time you stop to criticize,
Remember it you might.

THE LITTLE PYROMANIAC

He could always start a campfire
With just a match or two,
And flames would climb to twenty feet
Before that lad was through.
His father warned him many times
That fire was really hot,
But like too many boys these days
Listen, he would not.
He found a can of gasoline
High on a shelf, well hidden.
Got a ladder, brought it down,
Though he knew it was forbidden.
He took it to the outhouse,
Poured it down the pit.
"Eliminate the smell," he thought.
"That'll be the end of it."

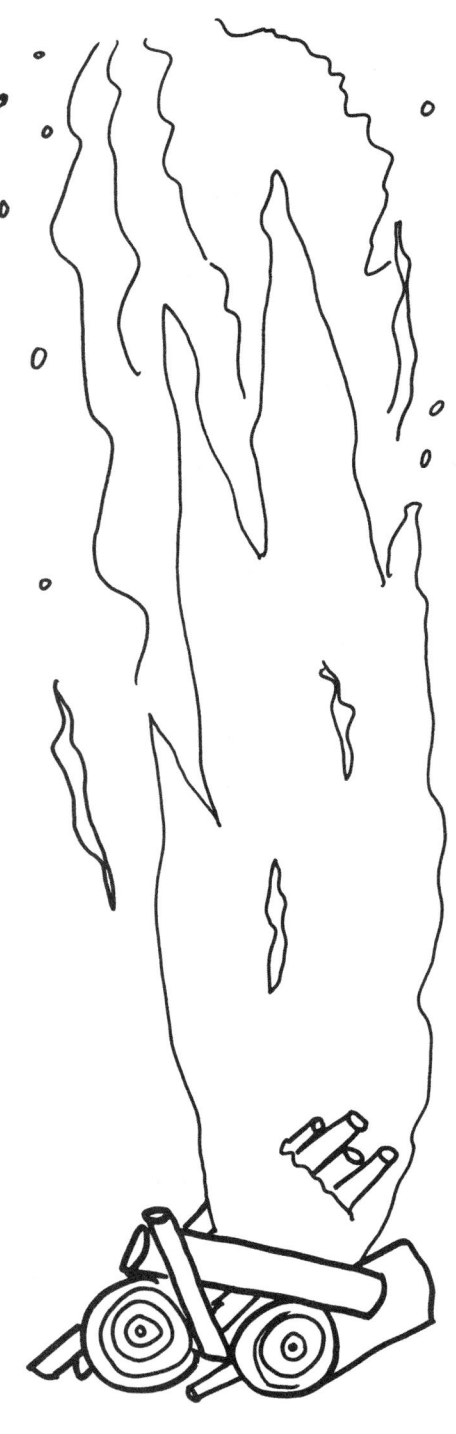

But when he tossed the match
The entire outhouse blew!
It layered all the field
And the little pyro, too.
Yes, he raised a stink that day,
One skill that he could master.
Follow rules! Don't play with fire!
Or you court your own disaster.

An extension of my fire building days as a Boy Scout...

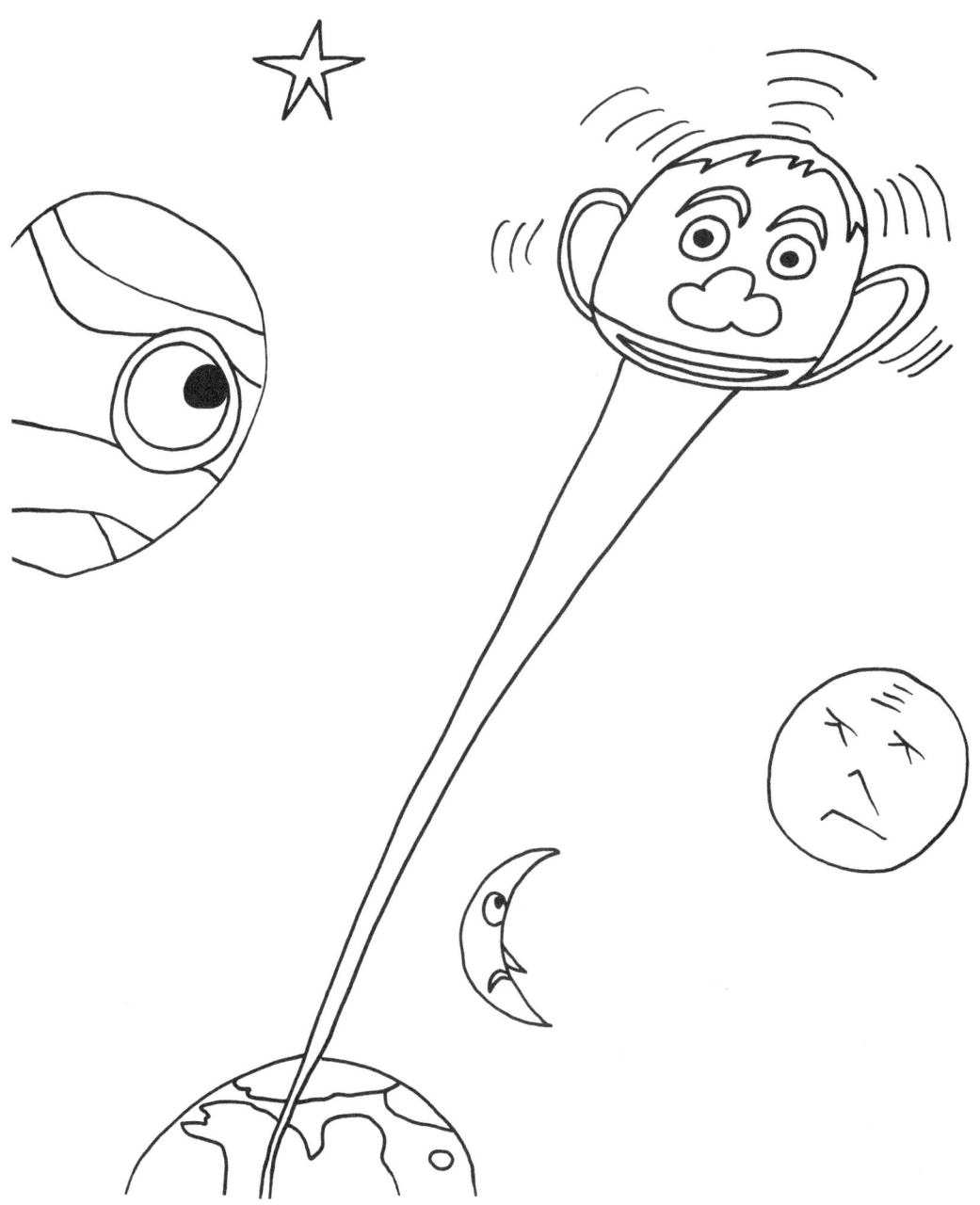

OLLIE, THE BOBBLE-HEAD BOY

Oliver, the Bobble-head boy,
Was never happy as a toy.
Wanted legs and feet to walk
And especially a tongue to talk.
A nearby fairy heard his wish.
Granted! (With a wandly swish!)
"Just one thing that you should know:
Tell a lie, your neck will grow!"
Ollie nodded (as he always did)
But let the lies flow from his lid.
Big ones! Small ones! So he grew
And told some more to birds that flew.
Reached up to a satellite!
Was on a TV show last night!
He told so many! Grew so fast!
He reached up to the moon and past!
On to Mars and Jupiter
Went the bobble Oliver.
No one talks to Ollie now.
(Those who want to don't know how!)
He tells his lies in outer space
But here or there it's still disgrace.
The consequences are no cure
Else we'd all tell the truth for sure!
(If from this tale you did not discern
This last line means SOME FOLKS DON'T LEARN!)

WALTER WUPPERMAN'S WINGS

They gathered along Texas Street
From top to bottom of the hill,
And as Walter stepped out from the walk
The crowd was hushed and still.
He was tall and skinny for his age
With arms especially long.
He had flapped his wings for weeks
To try to make them strong.
The bruises were still visible
From his last aborted goof,
But his cardboard wings had padded him
When he jumped off of the roof.

His wingspan was impressive
As he turned into the wind,
And the crowd all held its breath
As he started to descend.
Walter took those giant strides
And flapped with all his might.
If trying could have given lift
He would have taken flight.
When Walter reached the bottom
His arms were tired and sore,
And his mother seemed relieved
When he said, "I'll try no more!"
But everyone who watched him
Has remembered to this day
The time that Walter Wupperman
Tried to fly away.

This is a true story that happened during my father's childhood in Austin Texas in the 1930's.

TURNABOUT MOUNTAIN

"You've come far," the old man said,
"I'd even say done well.
But the final outcome's yet to be
And what comes next will tell.
Cast your eyes into the sunset,
To that highest mountain peak,
For unless you reach the top
You'll never gather what you seek.
Many have tried to pass that way,
So many I quit countin',
But most I see head back this way
When they come to Turnabout Mountain."

The old man shook his head,
Admitted, "Yes, I too once tried.
I almost made it to the top
But then the oxen died.
A blizzard came howling from the north
With twenty feet of snow.
Least that's how I remember it,
'Twas so long ago.
I'd go with you once again
If it weren't for all this doubtin'.
Afraid that's the thing that happens
When you turn back at Turnabout Mountain."

The old man turned about
And peered into the west.
I think he must have wondered
If in truth he'd done his best.
But his words deepened our resolve
That we would not be broken.
We made a promise with our eyes
Though not a word was spoken.
For such a fellowship as ours
There can be no accountin'.
It's all for one and one for all
To conquer Turnabout Mountain.

The blizzards came, the oxen died,
But we climbed while we had breath,
For our resolve was "it or us"!
We were in it to the death.
Each step was utter agony
But it felt worse to stop
And because we climbed together
We each made it to the top.
The dreams we had came true
With blessings like a fountain!
That's what happens when you stick it out
In spite of Turnabout Mountain.

That was many years ago
And now I too am old.
All are gone who climbed with me
And made that trip so bold.
Yet they live on in me
And we'll live on in you,
For when you see that distant peak
We know what you will do.
Like us you'll brave the danger
And we'll know it from the shoutin',
That you have made it to the top
And over Turnabout Mountain.

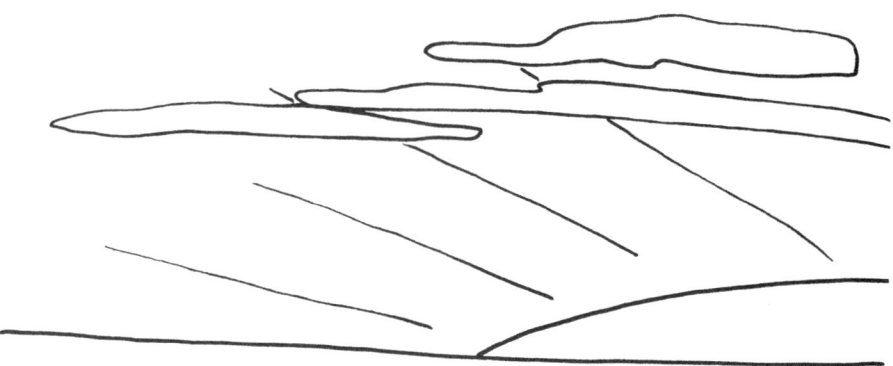

CLIMB THE RED MOUNTAIN

Only for an instant
Late in the waning year,
Only one place to see it
And I am standing here.
The leaves have turned from green
To orange, yellow, and brown,
And are red only on the mountain
Just as the sun goes down.
Beautiful beyond belief,
I am the only one who sees it!
This chance may come but a single time;
I must act now to seize it!
Climb the crimson mountain slopes
As the sun sinks low in the sky!
What will you find when you reach the top?
You won't know unless you try!

I saw this vision in Byrnes Mill, Missouri in 2002. It's the name of my second book.

ENDGAME

A king, a castle,
Just one pawn,
The queen, her court
Long since gone.
Alone these face
The fierce onslaught,
One last battle,
So many fought.

There is no rest
Through struggles long.
Fatigued and weary,
They must be strong.
All that's happened
Heretofore
For naught unless
They win one more.
On my mind
This game depends
And I'll be standing
When it ends.

Remembering my grandfather Alonzo Taylor and our chess matches.

IVAN THE TERRIER

A little bark, a tiny dog,
No bigger than a minute,
But play a game of tug-o-war
And that dog thinks he'll win it!
I lift the rope and there he hangs,
Rope clenched between his jaws!
He spins and wriggles in the air
Madly waving all four paws.
I set him down to see
If he'll finally give it up,
But he thinks he is winning now.
I'll have to show that pup!
I take the rope away,
Say, "NO! That's it!"
But though I think it's over
Ivan simply will not quit.
It's always the persistent one
Who wins our backyard game,
And if you don't give up your dreams
You'll find that life is just the same.
He's the smallest dog in any hunt
But his spirit knows no barrier.
Want to win against all odds?
Watch Ivan, the tenacious terrier!

IVAN THE TERRIER'S TAIL

Look at Ivan the terrier!
The dog has lost his tail!
We thought it might grow back
But hoped to no avail.
We called the man we bought him from.
He said to call the vet's
Who told us that his tail was gone
And one is all he gets.
What do they do with puppy tails
They've chopped off with a knife?
Ivan doesn't think of such;
He goes on with his life.
He wags the stub that he has left;
He runs around and plays.
Life's shorter than a terrier's tail
So be happy all your days.
Things that can't be changed,
Don't let them plague your mind,
Amazing things that we can learn
From a terrier's behind!

"Ivan the Terrier" was our rat terrier Neko. She never gave up.

TREED OFF

I don't think she'd ever been outside.
(It's a place she never goes.)
But there she was high in a tree!
How she got there no one knows.
That cat was wailing wildly.
It broke my heart to hear her cry.
Before I called the firemen
I thought I'd give it one good try.
I went and got a ladder,
Set it up against the tree,
Whispered softly to the cat,
"Don't worry now, it's me."
But the cat who'd warmed my lap
One many a winter's night
Somehow saw a snarling bear
And clawed at me in fright.
I drew my hand back quickly
But it was badly tattered!
I lost my balance, grabbed a branch,
For I was now unladdered.

And now just like the frightened cat
I could not get down.
The phone was in the house
And 'twas an hour's drive from town.
When the firemen finally came
The cat was calm and mellow,
But I was bleeding pretty bad
And my underwear was yellow.
Yes, I, too, can laugh about it now
But it surely wasn't fun,
And next time my cat gets in the tree
I'm calling nine-one-one!

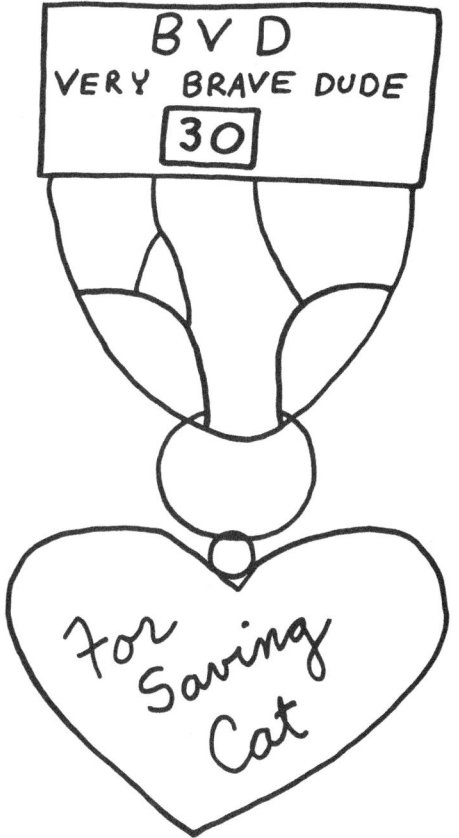

"Treed Off" started with scratches that our cat Star gave me when I tried to take her outside to see the birds.

THE DEAD SNAKE'S BITE

He dug it up. He had to see.
He found the severed head.
He touched it unafraid
For it was clearly dead.
He laughed to think how scared he was
When he heard its rattle near,
And put his finger in its mouth
To prove he had no fear.
He felt his heartbeat quicken
Though the snake could not attack.
He imagined it alive again
And drew his finger quickly back.

Alas! He touched the hanging tooth!
His finger snagged and bled.
He felt the venom's vicious gnaw
And then in fear, he fled.

Though you win the battle,
Taunting's never right.
When you dig up buried dangers
Expect the dead snake's bite!

This really happened near Wichita Falls, Texas on a campout in the early 1990's. No, it wasn't me.

THE BREATH HOLDING CONTEST

Just three feet of water,
Pretty hard to drown!
Who would need a breath first
And who would be the last one down?
Some came up in thirty seconds,
Most in just a minute,
And fifteen seconds later
Only two could win it.
They fought fire in their lungs
To a minute forty-five,
Then one came up for air
While the other took a dive.

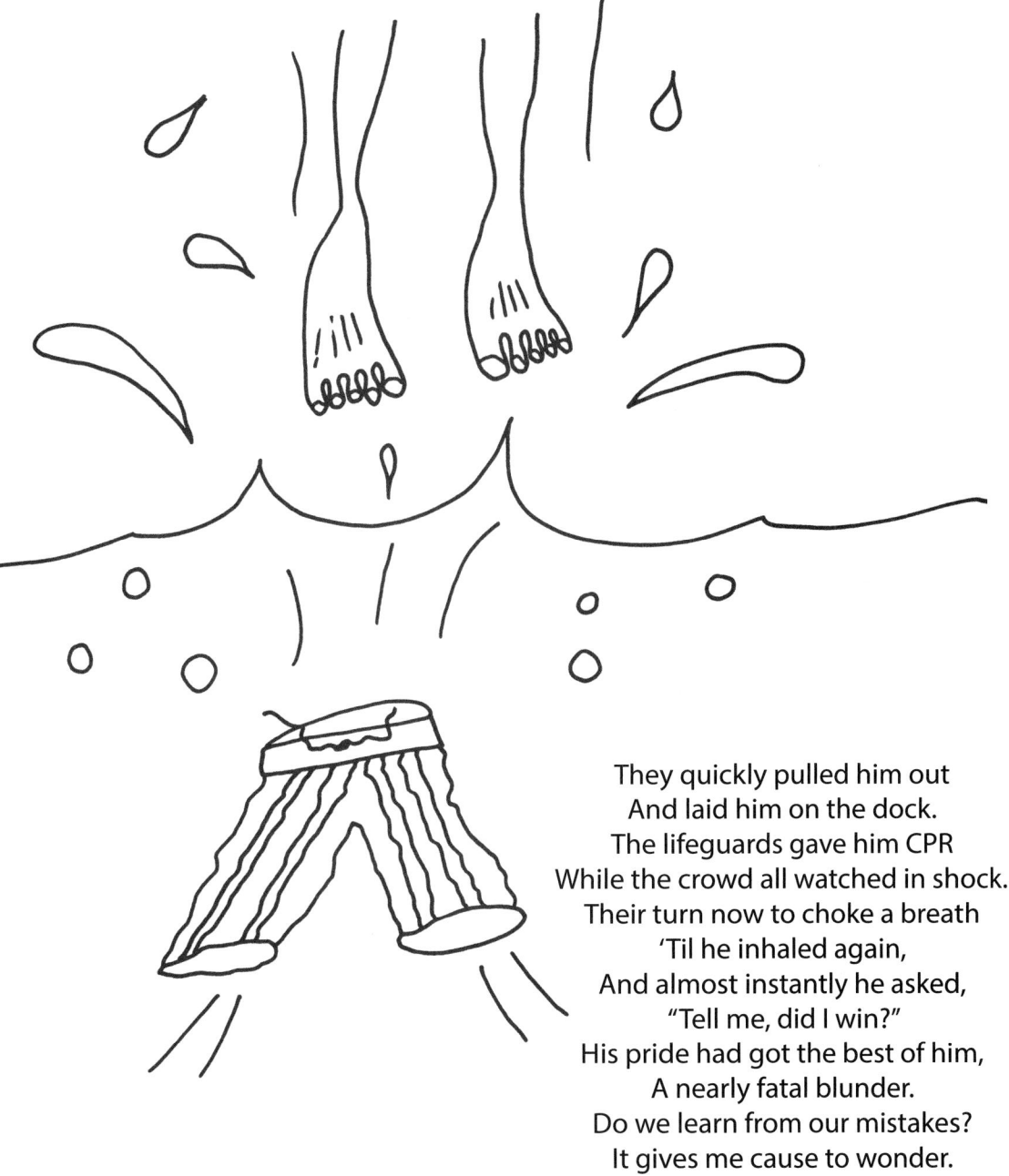

They quickly pulled him out
And laid him on the dock.
The lifeguards gave him CPR
While the crowd all watched in shock.
Their turn now to choke a breath
'Til he inhaled again,
And almost instantly he asked,
"Tell me, did I win?"
His pride had got the best of him,
A nearly fatal blunder.
Do we learn from our mistakes?
It gives me cause to wonder.

I actually saw this at a camp near Gallatin, Tennessee in the summer of 1987.

For this poem I combined a visit to the art museum in St. Louis in 2003 with my courtship of Sharon years earlier. The poem continues through page 43.

KING LOUIE'S HORSE'S BUTT: A LOVE STORY

An art museum for the fair,
Saint Louie in ought-four,
And a statue of His Highness
Like he's riding out the door.
The museum's full of treasures
From the Louvre and old King Tut
But as I leave I come face to face
With King Louie's horse's butt!

It doesn't seem appropriate
At his big tail to stare
And I wonder what they did
To get it so high up in the air.
A girl came up behind me.
She smiled so I said, "What?"
She said, "I think that yours is cuter
Than King Louie's horse's butt."

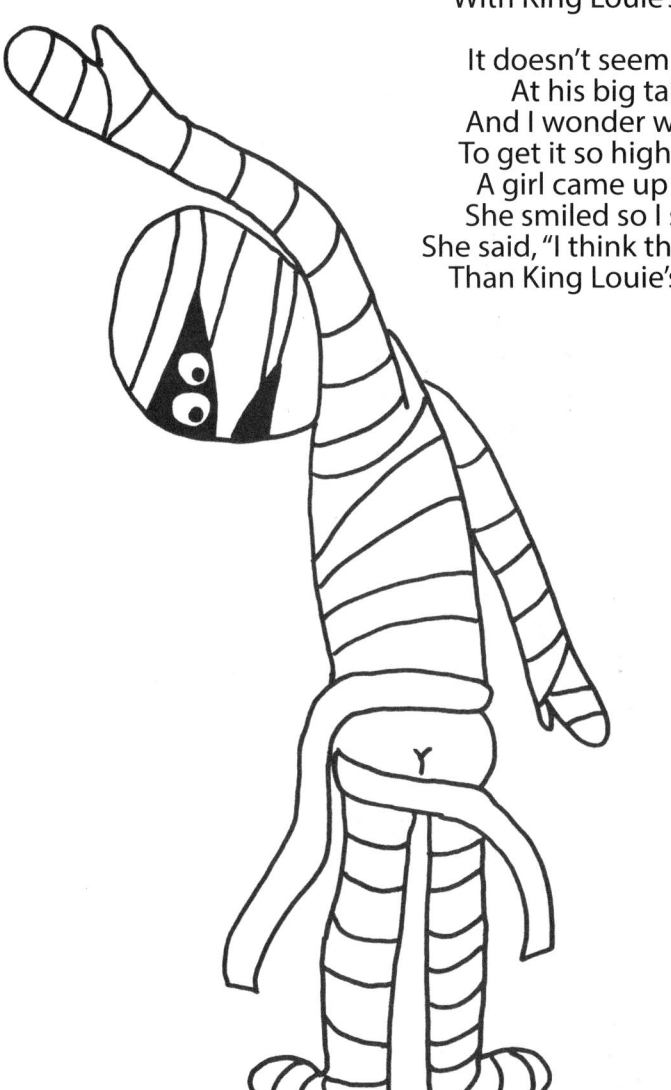

I was quite astounded
But I kind of liked the line
And when I got to know her
I vowed to make her mine.
We two think so much alike
As from one stone we're cut
So the two of us got married
Under King Louie's horse's butt!

We still visit the museum
And walk in Forest Park
And at night we hold each other's hands
And kiss there in the dark.
If I tell you where we like to kiss
You'll think that I'm a nut.
We stand in moonlit shadows
Of King Louie's horse's butt!

I know the statue will be there
When we are old and gray
For our love, like that old horse's butt,
Will never go away.
And on our anniversary
Up museum steps I'll strut
To kiss my wife and wave
At King Louie's horse's butt!

I wonder what we look like
From that pedestal above
And where our tale would rank
In the history of love.
But you would be quite lucky
Before life's book is shut
If you could have a love like ours
And King Louie's horse's butt.

THE FLATULENT FLUTIST

Of the stories I've told this one is the cutest
So hear ye the tale of the flatulent flutist.
When he played up an octave he lifted his leg.
"Play only the low notes!" the musicians would beg.
Rat-a-tat-tat was heard in the room.
It wasn't the drum but the flutist's perfume.
All in the orchestra cried as they played!
Crowds ran for the exits. Not a single one stayed.
The air grew dark in the orchestra pit.
For the conductor to see a candle was lit,
And just at that moment came a flatulent toot...

The last and the loudest note played on that flute!

I was a fradulent (not flatulent) flute player in middle school. I pretended to play but never let my flute make a sound because I couldn't keep up with the rest of the band.

THE EARTHWORMS

As I went jogging along the street
I looked down from the sun to my feet.
I saw an earthworm writhing in the heat
And all down the block the same scene repeat.
I stopped my hurried jogging pass,
Started tossing earthworms on the grass.
I picked them up one by one,
Saved them from the scorching sun.
My neighbor said from his lawn chair,
"Friend, what are you doing there?"
"Saving earthworms," was my reply,
"On the pavement they'll dry out and die."
My neighbor looked both left and right,
Said, "Friend, try as you might,
You can't possibly save all these earthworms today
And what difference would it make anyway?"
I paused and looked into my neighbor's eyes.
Said "Neighbor, here's what you need to realize:
It made a difference to that -"

SPLAT!
My neighbor squashed the earthworm flat!
He smashed another with his shoe,
Said, "Friend, there's something wrong with you.
I think you'd better go inside.
It's hot out here and your brain is fried!"

"The Earthworms" was my first funny and twisted poem and gave me a day's long belly laugh!

ROSES

Soft and velvet to the touch,
A beauty to the eye,
A fragrance sweetly gentle
With thorns that make you cry.
"Just so much like life,"
The philosopher supposes.
"I can live with thorns
But not without the roses."

KNOCKING ON PIPES

The woodpecker is loud today.
It's knocking on pipes again!
Why can't it stick to trees?
That's what the bugs are in!
It sure makes a ruckus,
Attracting my attention.
That pounding gives me headaches,
Migraines, and hypertension.
It does this every day!
It's just too much to bear.
And I can't escape it!
The sound goes everywhere.
And I wonder why it does that
For there is naught to gain.
It simply says, "I'm here!"
From the noise, that much is plain!
And as I sit and write these words,
Bits of poetry,
I start to realize
They are the pipes for me.

AN APOLOGY TO CAMELS

It has been pointed out to me
That I've maligned the camel.
To be sure it's not intentional
For it's such a noble mammal.
But, I see that I have erred,
Been badly in the wrong,
And to make it up to them
I'll sing the camel song:

I went riding on a camel
Into the desert sands!
The camel took me safely
Through these barren lands.
A fortnight without water,
I know, I did the math,
And my camel smells just fine
'Cause I haven't had a bath!

My camel is a friendly sort
To carry me around.
It's succeeded just three times
To throw me to the ground!
But it really is the social type,
It shares its friends with me.
There's only one big problem:
Its best friend is a flea!

I am proud of my nice camel.
It is my one true friend!
It helped me write this song
And gave it a good end.
For I had gone to thank it,
Bent over for some grass,
Then that nasty camel
Bit me on the...DON'T ASK!

BUT! Now I can't sit down!
No, you may not have a look!
Don't let your mother read this song
Or she'll throw away my book!

Our llamas are not camels. THANK GOD!

THE PATHS DIVIDE

You join us on our journey;
We greet you with a smile.
It's good to have someone like you
Walk with us a while.
You listen while we tell you things
That on our path we've learned.
We watch and marvel at your skill
And the honors you have earned.
Such a pleasant journey
And we wish it would not end,
But we can see our paths divide
As we come around the bend.
There are those who'll tell you
That from our path you must not stray,
But it is your path you walk
And it simply leads away.

But before we reach that junction
There is something we must do:
As your parents we just want to say
How much we think of you.
So hold our hands and talk with us
As we travel side by side.
We promise that we'll let you go
When the paths we take divide.
For somewhere on the road ahead
Our trails will once more touch,
And we'll say then as we do now,
"We love you, so very much."

"The Paths Divide" was written for our son Ryan's eighth grade graduation.

"Leading the Unicorn" was written because our daughter Erin liked unicorns. It led to my book ***Dale the Uniclyde.***

LEADING THE UNICORN

Free and wild, so beautiful,
The unicorn fills my dreams.
What joy 'twould be to catch it!
So close I am it seems.
And then it walks right up to me!
The reins are in my hands.
Its freedom and its faith are mine
As in front of me it stands.
With such power I am now endowed
To lead it through the land,
But the dream that is the unicorn
I do not yet understand.

For no matter how I try to lead
I cannot avoid its horn,
And I cannot lead my dreams
Anymore than this unicorn.
What then to do with this magic horse
That gave itself to me?
I take the bridle from its mouth
And let my dreams run free!
I touch the mystic horse of dreams
And its strength I feel inside.
I am one now with my unicorn
And where I go, I ride!

FIDDLE-DEE-DO

Fiddle-de-do, Fiddle-de-dee,
Oh if you could only see
All the things that trouble me
You could not ignore my plea
And at my side you'd quickly be.

Fiddle-de-dee, Fiddle-de-do,
Even though the rent is due
And the dollars are, well, far too few.
I don't have to tell a friend like you.
You've run away! I guess you knew.

A BUCKET OF SAND

A plastic shovel, two tiny hands,
A bucket filled with shells and sands.
The seagulls call, the child distract
But fly away when they're attacked.
Tiny footprints, that way, this,
The salty breeze, the ocean's kiss.
Memories of bygone days
Return to me with twilight's gaze.
Youth that did the ocean brave
Lost just like the fallen wave
And yet returning to the sea
There's a child who looks like me.
What magic in that tiny hand
That puts time into this pail of sand!

SANDALS

Easy on my feet,
Keep off sand that's hot.
Whenever it is warm
I wear mine a lot.
Sandals make toes happy
'Cause they can wiggle free.
Whenever I wear sandals
So can the rest of me.
No other kind of footwear
Can hold up any candles
To how I feel inside
Whenever I wear sandals.

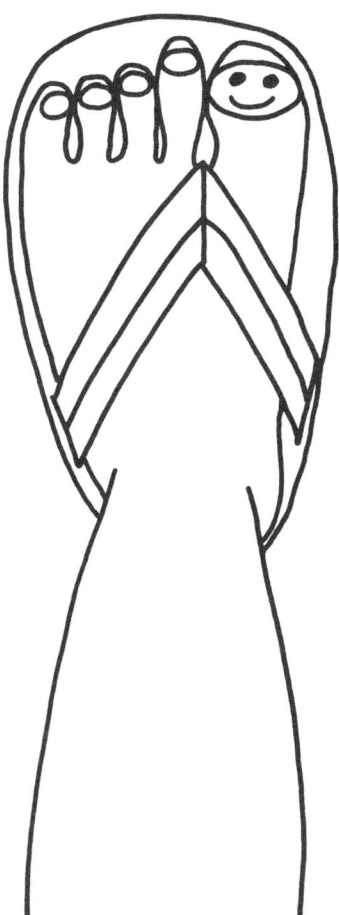

STUBBLE

White hair on my cheek,
Blacker on my chin,
Thicker than on top
Where it's become quite thin.
Wear it on the weekend,
Shave it Monday morn.
Have to go to work
All neat and newly shorn.
I suppose if I forgot
They'd think I was in trouble
But don't suppose I'm not
Just because I don't have stubble.

RAIN ON CANVAS

Rain on canvas comforts me
even though I'm wet.
It conjures up old feelings
that I never will forget.
For I remember days like this
when we went out to camp
and how our friendships grew
despite the cold and damp.
Someone made a fire
and sang a happy song
and with such company
nights didn't seem so long.

I heard the drumbeat playing
on my shelter's canvas roof
and a little on my sleeping bag
for it wasn't waterproof.
We talked the whole night through
right up to the dawn
and like our days of youth
the rain was quickly gone.
But I remember noises
that carry to this day
and the sound of rain on canvas
still takes me far away.

LAST CHANCE FOR THE BIG PURPLE DOG

"Today's the day." "She needs a home."
The officers' tones were grim
For they'd come to love that purple dog
And she in turn loved them.

But who would take a purple dog?
With such color it can't be well.
And can purple dogs be vicious?
At that time no one could tell.
Time had all run out
And no one took her yet
And the officer hung his head
As he got the phone to call the vet.
"I have a purple dog," he said,
"I'll bring her over in the van."
"Oh good!" said the happy vet,
"For I know a purple man."
It isn't always obvious
Like one's furry coated hue
But everyone needs a special friend
And there is one for you!

STUBBING MY TOE

I kicked a box and stubbed my toe
And now I'm watching where I go.
I'm walking very gingerly.
Does my toe control the rest of me?
It made me hop and made me yell
But what I said I'll never tell!
The only things I didn't do
Were move the box or wear a shoe,
For that would so defy convention,
Instead of cure to try prevention!

CHASE IT LIKE A SEAGULL

Gliding o'er the waters
Their voices call to me.
Oh, to be a seagull
And fly about, so free!
I'd soar into the dawn
And try to wake the sun
But first I'd strive to reach the stars
And eat them one by one!
If not, it wouldn't matter;
The sea has lots of fish.
To be fat and full and happy,
That's a seagull's wish!

And when the day is over
And the sun has passed on by,
I'd make a final charge
Into the fading sky.
For life is lived but once,
It offers no repeats,
So chase it like a seagull
As the evening sun retreats.
For when the night has fallen
And all the light has gone,
Even in the darkness
Your spirit still flies on.

PAUSE TO DREAM

As I wandered
down a path
I came upon a stream
and there I sat
to rest,
to ponder,
and to dream.
I listened to
the birds
(a gentle breeze
was blowing)
and thought about
important things
like where my life
was going.
Which way would
I be walking
if I were following
my heart?
And when better than
today
would be
the time to start?
And I watched
the water
wash away
leaves fallen
yesterday
and decided
it was best
to begin without
delay.

So I stood
and stretched,
and shook my head,
and looked around
once more,
picked up my things
and chose a path
different
than before.

A DIFFERENT PATH

I wandered down
a brand new path
that led
I know not where
and wondered
would I know the end
should I venture there.
Each turn,
each twist,
each step I took
led me somewhere
new
and there were places
grown so thick
that I could scarce get through.
And when I paused
to look
and plan my next
attack
I could hear
the voices
calling to
come back.
Swiftly then
I'd lift my feet
and quickly stride
ahead,
away from
old mistakes
to new mysteries
instead.

And then
the voices
faded,
my narrow trail
grew wide,
and suddenly
I felt my heart
as it beat
with joy
inside.

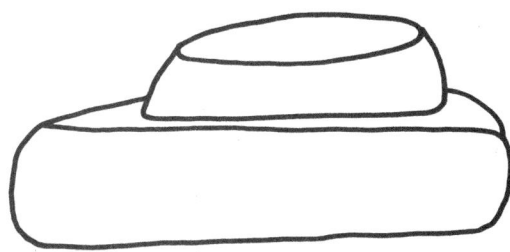

My friend and former Scoutmaster Charlie Nutter likes my poems but said I was still. . .

NOT SHAKESPEARE

You're not Shakespeare or Mark Twain.
You're not Shel or Dr. Seuss.
Your fables aren't like Aesop's
Or even Mother Goose!
Who do you think your are
To write in such a way?
You haven't suffered quite enough.
You've still got dues to pay!
The people smile and tell you
That you have talent, sure,
But when it come to buying
They almost all demure.
You'd better keep your day job
'Cause on this you can't subsist
And all the stories have been told.
There's not a one they've missed.

No, I am not Shakespeare
And I never was Mark Twain
But I have paid my dues in full
And had my share of pain.
Dr. Seuss is long since gone
And I no longer hear from Shel
But after Goose and Aesop
There still are tales to tell.
With my pencil and my paper
I'll give it my best try
And I guess if you are reading this
I succeeded, didn't I?
But I don't need a reason
To do this thing I do
'Cause I like to tell my stories
To folks I like, like you!

SHAKESPEARE FROG

He couldn't get the part.
He was too short for Romeo
So he tried out for Juliet
To get into the show.
It took a lot of makeup
But he finally looked okay
And decided he would pull a stunt
To blow the crowd away.

"I'll leap into my lover's arms
From atop the balcony
So when people think of Juliet
They will remember me!"
He had them build a platform
One hundred stories high
Neglecting one important fact
And that is: Frogs can't fly!

Shakespeare Frog! Oh, Shakespeare Frog!
We shall ne'er forget
For there never was a braver
Nor a flatter Juliet!

NO TV

If there were no TV
I think of all the things I'd see:
A flower bloom, a bird in flight.
Without TV I even might
Go outside of my front door
Where I could see a whole lot more.
People going all about!
Why I could even venture out
On a walk or in my car
But I'll never know just how far
I might have, could have, should have gone
'Cause I've still got the TV on!

CLUTTER

I wish there were
Some words to utter
To help get rid
Of all this clutter.
Bags and boxes
Everywhere
On the sofa
And the chair.
Cans and bottles
Gotta go!
Clean and sparkly!
Make it so.
Clutter's gone
Just like that!
But where I wonder
Is the cat?

OLD CHEESE

When I woke up this morning
My stomach said, "Eat!"
And my tongue said, "I want more
Than mushy oat bran or wheat!"
And so I went searching
In my refrigerator
And found some old cheese
Down deep in its core.
The date was expired.
It was sixteen months old
But I got out a knife
And scraped off the mold.
It looked a lot better
And tasted like new
But I was still hungry
So I ate the rest, too.
Now some folks might call that
Stupid or dumb
But you're holding your stomach.
Are you hungry?

WANT SOME?

THE TALKING FEET

I had a very weird dream.
My feet began to speak!
They complained about their bunions
And how my ankles creak.
They said my shoes were fitted
At least a size too small
And demanded a massage
Or they wouldn't walk at all.
They asked for thicker socks
To stay warm in icy weather
And sandals for the summertime
Instead of wearing leather.
When I finally woke
I took my morning walk
Thankful for my pair of feet
And glad that they can't talk.

I used to entertain Erin and Ryan with my talking feet. Silly, but better than stinking!

THE PIG AND THE POODLE

I have a pig and a poodle
I keep in the house and sty.
It's the poodle that stays in the house
With the pig left to wonder why
It has to stay on the outside
In the rain, the heat, and the snow,
While I pamper the powderpuff poodle
To take to the kennel club show.
But it really shouldn't be jealous
For an indoor visit awaits,
At breakfast tomorrow morning
And we're using the best china plates!

Inspired by clouds near Springfield, Missouri and by our love of bacon.

PINCHING THE DINOSAUR

Have you ever tried to pinch
An angry dinosaur?
A caveman told me once
It was quite an awesome chore.
The reason that he did it
Was just to hear them roar
But I don't think he pinches
Or hears them anymore.

The kids wanted a dinosaur poem. Now I have lots of them in my book, ***The Dinosaur's Lingerie.*** And I write about "The Chubby Dinosaur!" a lot!

JUAN PABLO MADRID

This is the tale of Juan Pablo Madrid
Who amazed us all with the things that he did.
He took on the rapids at Niagara Falls,
Climbed and rappelled on China's Great Walls.
In all that he did he surely was brave
But what mattered most was the love that he gave.
Love of life and the trust of his friends,
The good in these gifts just never ends.
So on top of a mountain or sailing the sea
In every adventure I'll remember J. P.
For courage and valor he had in excess
And for his example I carry no less.
Truly he was a magnificent man
Whose deeds proclaimed loudly these words:
"Yes! I can!"

THE PIG HAS WINGS

The pig has wings.
They're little things
But high up in the air it swings
And I think of all the many kings
Who would have given crowns and rings
If they could rise up as on strings
Like the little pig with wings.

THE FIRST DAY BACK

I hate to get up in the morning
On the very first day of school.
I spent the whole summer playing
Without following one single rule.
But now those days are over
And I'm finding my way to my room.
With each step I'm feeling a sense
Of impending and awful doom.
I pause to ponder a question
As I put my hand to the door:
If this is what my life has become,
Do I want to live anymore?
I accept my fate with a sigh
For all good things must pass,
Walk in, put my books on the desk
And say, "Welcome! Good morning, class!"

I DON'T LIKE COFFEE!

I don't like coffee!
I don't like tea!
They just don't taste
That good to me.
I won't drink 'em!
Not one sip.
If they're too hot
They'll burn my lip!
Why'd they make
Drinks so bitter?
It tastes like they
Used kitty litter!
But it's so hard
To get up.
Think I'll have
A second cup!

"I Don't Like Coffee!" said my wife Sharon. I do, and I need it, too!

THE ALGEBRA POEM

Algebra, algebra!
Do you know the answer? Duh!
x and y and z and q!
Look at how my problems grew!
Should I times it or divide
Or add a bit to either side?
What kind of person writes this stuff?
Weren't fractions bad enough?
Stick to numbers! Can the words!
Algebra is for the birds!

This poem and "The Pythgorean Poem" enshrine my daughter Erin's struggles with math. Her grandpa Dale was a math genius. Go figure!

THE PYTHAGOREAN POEM

Pythagorus, Pythagorus!
Why'd you sick this plague on us?
Squaring sides and squaring 'nooses!
Teachers taking no excuses.
Are your square roots all exact?
Ask again and you'll get smacked!
Did you calculate, I wonder,
How many feet of dirt you're under?
I square the sides - that's ninety-three -
Still not deep enough for me!

SHARKS TO CHASE

I chased a shark the other day.
I thought it might be fun to play.
But it turned 'round and opened wide
And – just like that! – I was inside.
Life's like that when you live on credit
So take your card out – NOW! – and shred it!

This poem and "Fiddle-dee-do" made me laugh when money was tight as it is so very often for poets, and for others.

OUR EAGLE

He's been stretching wings
Since the day he first breathed air
And every time he conquered one
He'd find another dare.
One more challenge to pursue
And chase it to the end
– His fierce determination! –
On that we could depend.
And now those wings are ready!
Our son is fully grown.
He has felt his freedom now
And to such heights he's flown.
And on this day and from this place
His journey starts anew
And though we can't go with him
The path he chose is true.
Honor, courage, faith,
He carries these things high.
Our son flies as an eagle!
There are no limits in his sky.
And so we proudly watch
As he rises on those wings
In thanks and admiration
For our son who does these things.

THEREIN WAS THE DAWN

He'd never spent so much time
So far away from home
Where the body and the spirit
Each had room to roam.
And somewhere on a mountainside
Way off the beaten track
A boy realized he was a man
And there was no turning back.
It might have been the eagle
High in the azure blue,
Advising him his set of wings
Must make his dreams come true.
It could have been the bear
That brushed the tent at night,
Reminding him to treasure
The gift of morning light.
And it might have been the sunrise
That crept up mountain slopes
That said to him great deeds would come
If he'd act upon his hopes.
And so he did and followed
That light up to the peaks
And now he knows that with his best
He can reach the goals he seeks.
He's traveled many miles since then
As days have come and gone
But a man awoke as daylight broke
And therein was the dawn.

IT'S TOO SMALL

It's too small but he still wears it,
Fading, but he doesn't care.
In fact, I think, of all he has
It's his favorite thing to wear.
He wore it every day at camp,
Made me wash it every night.
Wasn't that just yesterday?
How did it get so tight?
A craft he made sits on his shelf,
His very own creation.
It was fun to watch him work,
So full of concentration.
He shot a bow and arrow
And even learned to swim
But the friendships that he made
Still mean the most to him.
I have a shirt just like his
And though it's fading, too,
It reminds of times together
And those great days we knew.
So when he wears that tattered shirt
I don't really mind at all.
It represents the things he learned
That helped him grow so tall.

This poem and "Our Eagle" were written for our son, Ryan, an Eagle Scout.

WHY PHYLLIS BURNED THE BARN

She calmly led the horses out.
The cows and pigs were next
But why she left the hay inside
Left us all perplexed.
She said it was intentional
Which we couldn't understand.
How could such a perfect girl
Behave so out of hand?
They asked her at the station
And she told them straight away
It was because she had heard
Snakes were in the hay.
Now we all have our blind spots
And idiosyncrasies
But if there's a snake inside our house
Could you just TELL me, please?

Commemorating a comment by my friend Phyllis Young who does not like snakes.

"Cookies by a Zombie?" I asked my daughter Erin. I thought she said that. She thought I was weird.

COOKIES BY A ZOMBIE

The words were very strange.
I paused and shook my head.
Why would someone bake a cookie
If he or she were dead?
Digestion wouldn't work
And you surely couldn't taste!
I wonder that a Zombie
Would have such time to waste.
So I had a conversation
With the Zombie down the street
Who told me that a cookie
Was more than just to eat.
"It really is an art," it said,
"Like baking poetry,"
But when I read my poem
Here's what it said to me:
"As a Zombie I am dead
But still I am no dummy
And your poem's like a cookie
Because it's very crumby!"

STANDING ON BOXES

I'm standing on boxes
On top of a chair
Two hundred feet
High up in the air!
And I ponder this question
In my altitude rare,
"Do you have a parachute
Or a ladder to spare?"

"Standing on Boxes" reminds me to use the right tool for EVERY job!

"Butterfly Wings" came to me as I was driving! I had to park and write the poem before it flew away!

BUTTERFLY WINGS

A poem is a moment
caught like a butterfly.
You have to let it land
for you'll hurt it
if you try
to catch it in a net
or
trap it in a jar.
Words apart so common
now brought together
are
so fragile
and so beautiful
like a butterfly's new wing
and from cocoons
placed in my mind
I love to watch them spring.

WARRIOR IN THE LAND OF KINGS

I'm a warrior in the land of kings
But I won't kneel and kiss their rings
For I'm the one the people follow,
A fact that kings find hard to swallow.
And though besieged on every side
I would rather fight than hide.
For I know that victory's mine
If not in these realms, those divine!
For a warrior rules not by decrees
But through the souls his battle frees.
The warrior fears not for his fate.
His courage is what makes him great.
And when the final trumpet's blown
I'll be upon the highest throne
For in the end one truth remains:
In the land of kings, the warrior reigns!

Inspired by comments by Dave Guckes
and in tribute to my father, Dr. Dale von Rosenberg,
a warrior to his final breath
whose spirit lives stronger now more than ever

MAY YOUR LIPS ALWAYS BE LONG ENOUGH

May your lips always be long enough
To kiss the ones you love.
May your skies always be bright enough
To lift your eyes above.
May your hands always be strong enough
To hold on to what's good
Yet wise enough to let things go
When your heart says that you should.
May your feet always be sure enough
To find the narrow way
And kind enough to those you love
To bring you home someday.
May your heart always have courage
Enough to carry on
When hands and feet have failed
And all your strength is gone.
May your spirit then be bold enough
To look to that bright sky
And fill your soul with faith enough
To give you wings to fly!

I sign my children's book **I Don't Want to Kiss a Llama!** with the first two lines of this poem.

COURAGE IS ITS OWN REWARD

Toil and trouble, fear and pain,
Can I stand when powers wane?
With this answer my mind fills:
"Courage dared always instills
An attitude of 'Yes! Can do!'
That human spirit does renew.
A habit stronger, now restored,
Courage is its own reward!"

Do I quit or do I stick
When the battle's going thick?
And failing first is it I
Who then will give a second try?
Better, stronger, once again,
Determination full to win
As through the fray I sound this chord:
Courage is its own reward.

I look up to the mountain peak
For it's such goals I constant seek.
Weary yet no pause to rest
For there is joy in such a test.
To my limit, stretching past,
Exhilaration! Here at last!
Whatever goal I'm aiming toward,
Courage is its own reward!

What, to me, do these words mean?
A different outlook I have seen!
Ends and outcomes change for me
When with courageous eyes I see.
The path through life steep and rough
Yet heart of courage is enough
To serve as both my shield and sword.
Courage is its own reward.

All do strive for earthly gain
But in the end just these remain:
Honor, courage, faith and love!
For such ideals rise far above
All the things to have and hold.
Oh, for courage to be bold
To measure these as life is scored.
Courage is its own reward.

MY TEACHER'S UNDERPANTS

When I was at the store downtown
I happened, just by chance,
To see my teacher buy (on sale!)
A dozen underpants.
Some were checkered, some were plaid,
Some were polka-dotted,
And it seemed to me that twelve is more
Than teachers are allotted.
I never thought that teachers
Gave thought to underwear,
Much less that they would decorate
Their bu- -! Excuse me, derriere.
Oh, that I could wipe away
Those thoughts deep in my mind
Like what is in between
My teacher's trousers and behind!
It wrecks my concentration!
My grades are falling so
And I've decided that's one thing

I JUST DON'T WANT TO KNOW!

SPOT, THE TALKING BUG

I thought I'd left the TV on
But the noise came from the rug
Where I made acquaintance first
With Spot, the talking bug.
I picked him up and held him
In the palm of my right hand
As he proceeded to regale me
With discourse glib and grand.
At first the softest whisper,
His voice began to boom
Moving my emotions
And sending tremors through the room.
He made me laugh! He made me cry!
Such vision he portrayed
Inspiring me to action,
A man and bug crusade!
I was in his hand
As he was deep in mine
And I rose up to my feet
To hear his last opine.
Yet so impassioned was I,
My manners I forgot
And clapped my hands together –
How rude! Sorry, Spot!

"Spot, the Talking Bug" lived and died in a dream I had.

MY BUTLER

He wakes up at the break of dawn
And starts his daily chores,
Tiptoes very quietly
And softly closes doors.
He gets the paper, takes out trash,
Turns the TV on
And starts a load of dishes –
All this before it's dawn!
He feeds the dogs. He feeds the cats.
He cleans the kitty litter
But he says he's going to quit
If we get another critter!
He drives my daughter to her school
And goes to get our mail.
He shovels snow in wintertime,
The driveway without fail!
He mows the grass in summer
And rakes up leaves in fall.
Without my butler I don't know
If the house would stand at all!
My wife thinks that it's great
Since my butler works for free
But I don't like it half as much
Because my butler's me!

"My Butler" is a response to an inquiry
about the size of my household staff.

NEANDERTHAL NED

Neanderthal Ned had a club in one hand
And in the other he held a gold wedding band.
He came up behind Nell to tap her soft head
But she twisted around and here's what she said.
"You'd better learn manners, you big bellied brute!
Shave! Lose some weight! Wear a tie and a suit!
Learn how to read, you big hairy dope,
And take a good bath! This time use the soap!"
Ned gave her the ring and went down to one knee.
The result of this meeting's now quite clear to me.
I'm bathing at home and learning at work
And changing the diapers! Am I a big jerk!
It's not now enough to bring home the bread.
I have to be sensitive! Thanks a lot, Ned!

THANK YOU CANDLE CHARM

They have lily of the valley
And perfume of the rose.
Candle Charm has scents
To cheer up every nose!
Get one as a present
To help a friend get well
Or give someone a hint
About a better way to smell.
I finally got the message.
(I have one beneath each arm!)
And my wife and all my friends say,
"Thank you, Candle Charm!"

THE POET LAUREATE OF BYRNES MILL

I want to be the laureate
of the Village of Byrnes Mill,
A position I will take
Since there's no one else who will.
I'll regale you with my stories
And astound you with my rhymes.
I've asked if you would hire me
About a hundred times.
I'll take the job for nothing
And give you twice as much.
Think how good our town would be
With my poetic touch!
And now the drum roll starts!
It's voting time again.
The mayor went home sick
So this time I might win.
He argued and he hollered
Until his face turned blue
But now I'm poet laureate
By a vote of three to two!

I really AM the *poet laureate* of Byrnes Mill, Missouri!

A WHOLE NEW TURN

Oh, the twists and turns of fate
That mark us either poor or great!
Do events we don't control
Consign us to a certain role?
Or are we somehow greater than
A pawn in someone's cosmic plan?
Do I quit or do I try
When my ventures go awry?
For should I one more time begin
'Twill be a stronger go therein,
One to change the distant stars,
A better future to be ours!
With grand affairs I will contend
To see them to a different end
For when I strive the things I learn
Give my life a whole new turn.

OF COLANDERS AND CALENDARS

I thought about the difference
Between these disparate things
As I met the New Year
With the musing that time brings.
I pondered on the colander,
How most things pass right through
And realized that with calendars
That's what happens, too.
Which things are important?
What items will I keep?
With colander and calendar
I pluck them from the deep!
And look at how they shine
And sparkle in the light,
The gems of truth and knowledge,
So precious in my sight!

ALL THE TEA IN CHINA

All the tea in China!
All the cats in Siam!
The gold in ol' Fort Knox!
That's how in love I am.
I used to think that I could be
In love – oh, just a little! –
But now I've lept the fence
Without stopping in the middle.
It's a whole new attitude
That's inside me now
And the police say I feel better
Than the local laws allow.
It's all because of you,
Your smile, your laugh, your touch!
And because you told me
You love me twice as much!
For all the cats in Siam
And all of China's tea
Don't mean half as half as much
As does your love for me!

SHARE A DREAM

Have a seat
beside me
as the sun begins to set
and we'll talk
of things to be
that haven't happened
yet.
The outcome of your dreams
that are so brave
and bold
and of mine
that are the same
though
I have grown quite old.
You have life
ahead of you
much more
than do I
but the dreams
I have are beautiful
just like
the evening sky.
They are in need
of younger hands
that will live
to greet the morn
for only in
another's heart
can they be
reborn.

If you can see
the beauty
in the moon's
soft beams
then take them through
the night
to the morning
of
your dreams!
Let the dream of freedom,
beauty, honor,
peace,
be the guiding force
that gives your life
increase.
And when
the sun has set
no longer
think of me
but of the dreams
we shared
and how
the world should be.

OLD SCHEMA

I wonder at the darkened stairs,
The cracks and pealing paint.
The school I used to think so new
Today seems rather quaint.
The halls where I once roamed,
The teachers I once knew,
All seem somewhat worse for wear
Yet I am older, too.
And the questions I once asked here
That I thought had gone for naught
Were answered in the lessons
That outside these walls, life's taught.
And so it's safe now to return
For what have I to fear?
The sticker that I wear
Says I just visit here.
Looking back, I should have worn
Such a sticker every day
To remind that life, like days at school,
Does surely slip away.
And so the gray-haired gentleman
Walks out the door again,
Smiles and wishes all the best
For the students walking in.

SEAGULL FOR A DAY

If I could be a seagull but only for a day
I wouldn't work at all. I'd just fly around and play.
I'd catch the ocean breezes and soar into the sky,
Thankful that for just one day I had wings to fly!
I'd scan the far horizon and try to bring it near.
Maybe I would rather be seagull for a year!
But that's enough of dreaming. I have work to do right now.
Seagull for a minute is all that they allow.
And yet we went together on a little ride
So part of me will always be a seagull deep inside.
Yes, seagull for a minute in this body I call me
Is sufficient for my spirit to live forever free!

Seagull poems remind me of the beach and my first book, **Don't Feed the Seagulls.**

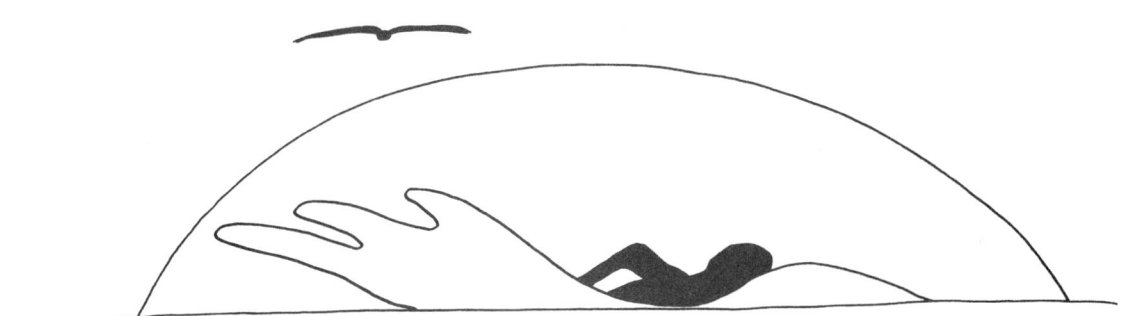

SPIRIT AND MEMORY

I've been told
I write a lot
about the nasty
bills I've got.
People think
it's way too much
and that I have
the Midas touch.
Sure! I might
sell you a book
but what about
the loans I took
to help us go
when we were sad
or cure us of
the ills we had?
Not to mention
printing cost
and how last year
we almost lost
our house, our home,
our wedding rings
yet we would sacrifice
these things
to tell a poem
here to you
and watch you smile
when I got through.
For what is life
if not the grace
to give up what
we can replace
for things that live
eternally
in spirit and
in memory?

LIGHT BLUE ALPACAS

Light blue alpacas
Are happy, it seems,
Or that's what they told me
Last night in my dreams.
They fly in a flock
Or is it a herd?
When I say it out loud
It sounds so absurd!
But I think of alpacas
And llamas a lot
Which makes people wonder
If I'm crazy or not.
Imagination, I say,
Is a wonderful thing
From whence light blue alpacas
Suddenly spring.
But my doctor says should
They return for a visit
He's bringing a net.
Hey!
That's not for me,

IS IT?

After a visit from the Light Blue Alpacas at the I Don't Want to Kiss a Llama! Store.

It was the name of a group of girls at a local school given them by their math teacher.

OVER AND OVER

You say that we must fight
And one of us must lose
But there are other options
That I would rather chose.
For I have come to realize
The price we each will pay
And so ask you one more time
If there's not another way
Since both of us must lose
For one of us to win,
A lesson man forgets
Over and over again.

TOO MUCH TO HANDLE

The bank that charged me late fees, thousands by the minute,
Had to close its doors! There was no money in it.
The one that turned me down for too low a credit score
Was shut down by the fed and they're not open anymore.
The card that charged percentages higher than my age
Had its CEO locked up in a cage.
And I wonder how it is that I with income mediocre
Am being asked to pay to re-employ my broker.
I'm told that we all need them. They really know their trade!
So how is it they didn't save a dime from what they made?

What'd they do with all that money?
Was it just too much to handle?

Unfettered greed has always
And will always lead to scandal.

Anybody remember 2008?

AS IS

Dining room chairs in the basement,
Boxes of books in the hall!
The dishwasher's making some noises
But it's not cleaning at all.
The cats and the dogs just keep shedding!
Their hair's on the carpet like snow.
There are only twenty-four hours
Then the realtor's coming to show.
The grass has to be cut.
The walls need to be painted.
When my wife went to clean up the bathroom
She opened the door and just fainted!
Yet tomorrow it has to be sparkling
And looking exactly like new
So if you'd take it just as it is

I'd probably give it to you!

EIGHTEEN DOCTORS

I talked to eighteen doctors seeking their advice
and each one recommended I visit at least twice.
And so I changed my schedule, saw a doctor every day!
You should have seen the bills that I had to pay!
But I'm sure that it was worth it for each doctor was degreed
and it would have been an easy choice had any two agreed.

"Surgery!" "Holistic!"
"Medication." "Wait!"
"Take another test.
I must evaluate!"

Eighteen different doctors and thirty-six opinions
not including nurses, orderlies and minions.
So the choice is up to me and I don't know a lick
except this bit of wisdom:

"YOU'D BETTER NOT GET SICK!!!!"

"Eighteen Doctors" is how many of them my friend Wilma Addison had to see before she got well.

BLINDERS ON HORSES

They put blinders on horses
To restrict what they see
But horses don't wear them
When they're running free.
And I wonder what I'd do
Or what I might be
If I could take off the blinders
That they've put on me.

ADVICE FROM MY AUNT WINNIE

The advice from my Aunt Winnie
When my ears were turning red
Was clear, concise, and firm:
"Put that cap back on your head!"
But it wasn't only practical.
She was kind and wise
And the words she said could often
Take you by surprise.
There was the time I lost
My very favorite toy
And she knew just what to say
To help that little boy.
"I've looked everywhere," I said,
"That it could ever be!"
"Then look somewhere it couldn't!"
And her words helped me to see
Not only just the toy I found
But other things as well:
Ideas, dreams and meaning
In the stories I now tell.
"Dare to think and dare to dream
And seek out your own way!"
Advice from my Aunt Winnie
I've followed to this day.

"Advice from my Aunt Winnie" includes sayings and wisdom from my Mom's older sister, Winnifred Taylor Laubach.

TWO MORE FIDDLES

With two more fiddles I might find a string for one right note
Or strike upon a melody as good as any goat.
I could simulate the sound of squeaking brakes.
(Two would do it better but one is all it takes.)
I could get an innocent to admit to crimes galore
As long as I would promise not to fiddle anymore.
Music has a power given by the gods
But harmony and fiddles are constantly at odds.
I tried to teach a thousand applicants to play.
I failed! But with a fiddle it doesn't matter anyway!
Beneath the harvest moon I fiddled through the night.
That's what made the cow jump over it in fright!
With two more fiddles I could start a music revolution
And if you want me not to play you'll make a contribution.
You'd better dig down deep and find a lot to give
'Cause I've got two more fiddles . . .

. . . AND I KNOW WHERE YOU LIVE!

"Two More Fiddles" comes from a joke that a staff member at Silver Dollar City told me at a book signing there.

THERE'S AN OUTHOUSE IN BYRNES MILL

On the top of a hill here in Byrnes Mill
An ancient outhouse stands
Where you can sit and look beyond
To many far off lands.
To India and China,
To Nome and Timbuktu,
People's thoughts go wandering
And I find that mine do too.
But as I peer into the vastness
Of those skies away out yonder
My contemplation's personal
For it's closer things I ponder.
Indeed the pressing question,
The one thing I must know
E'er I leave this rustic throne is,

"Where'd the paper go?"

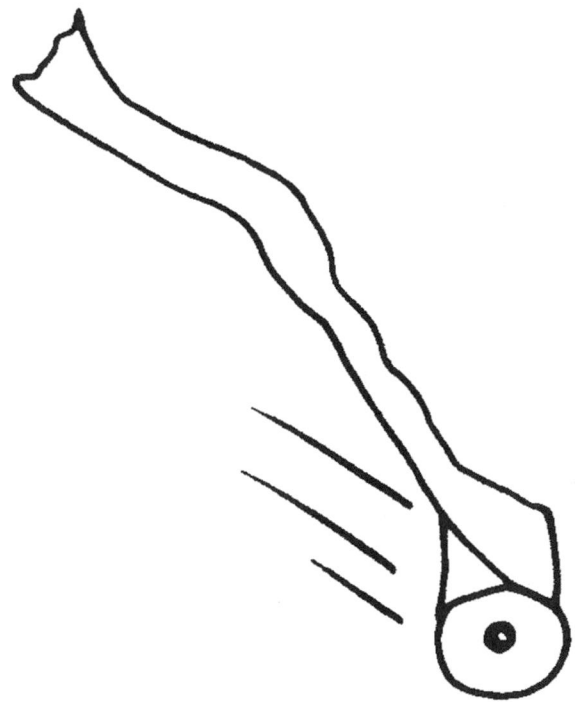

"There's an Outhouse in Byrnes Mill" but it finally fell over. Very sad! I am still the poet laureate of Byrnes Mill anyway.

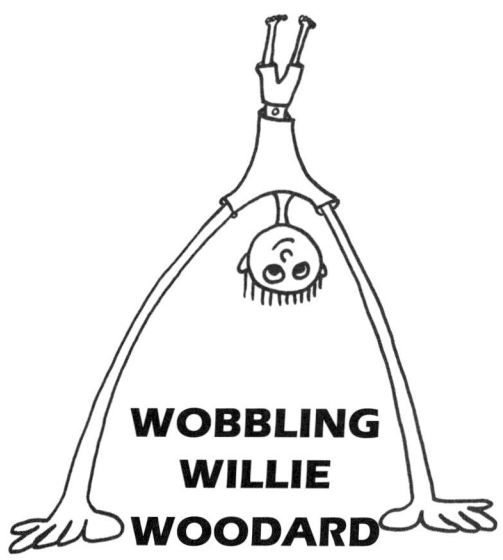

WOBBLING WILLIE WOODARD

It's a wonder Willie Woodard never came to fame
Though it's only through coincidence that we now know his name.
He was quite an acrobat, the best in his whole town,
And he walked upon his hands to see things upside down.
But there were lots of people who did not understand.
They shuffled feet and kicked to stir up dust and sand.
Willie sneezed and shook his head to recover from the shock
Then sought the higher ground and climbed the steeple clock.
They came from every house and farm for many miles around
Calling up to Willie, "Get back down on the ground!"
And Willie, when he saw them there chose that time to speak.
"Listen loud and clear," he said, "before you call me freak!
The things I say and do seem to be so strange
But I propose that each of us might need to make a change.
Show some understanding to different folks like me
And if you can't do that, perhaps just let them be.
Try to be a friend and they might be one back
And help you on some distant day when you're under like attack.
Together we might build a better world and town
And since we can't all fit up here I'll be coming down."
With that he tumbled nimbly back onto his feet.
Quickly he descended and joined the crowd there on the street.
And that's the last we've heard of wobble-walking Will
But the words he spoke that day give us guidance still.

DETERMINATION DEEP

Today I met a statue
That looked just like my son
And wondered of the life he led
And all the things he'd done.
And though he could not speak
And tell me what he knew
He made me pause a moment
To try the other shoe.
So young and full of confidence
To seek his wealth and fame
Like me so many years ago
And my son who does the same.
Did he have an inkling
Of the perils that befell?
The past much like the future
Hides and does not tell.
Yet in that face and in those eyes
There is determination deep,
A look that says that I have found
A single dream to keep.
What mystery is this
That his face appears again?
Yet so it is with all the dreams
Deep in the hearts of men.

The bust is in the St. Louis Museum of Art in Forest Park. It is dated ~600 A.D.

WHEN THE LAST CLOUD'S PAST

What happens when the last cloud's past
To reveal the bright full moon?
Does it portend clear skies ahead
Or a new storm coming soon?
When will the last wave hit the beach
And the ocean's pounding cease?
Will there ever be a time
When all on earth know peace?
Who will be the person
To think one last thought of hate?
Can you change your way of thinking
Or is it much too late?
For as the waves bear down again
And press on waiting sands
You have the answer to that question
Right there in your hands.
Now that the final cloud is past
What will the heavens do?
Look inside your heart and mind
For that depends on you.

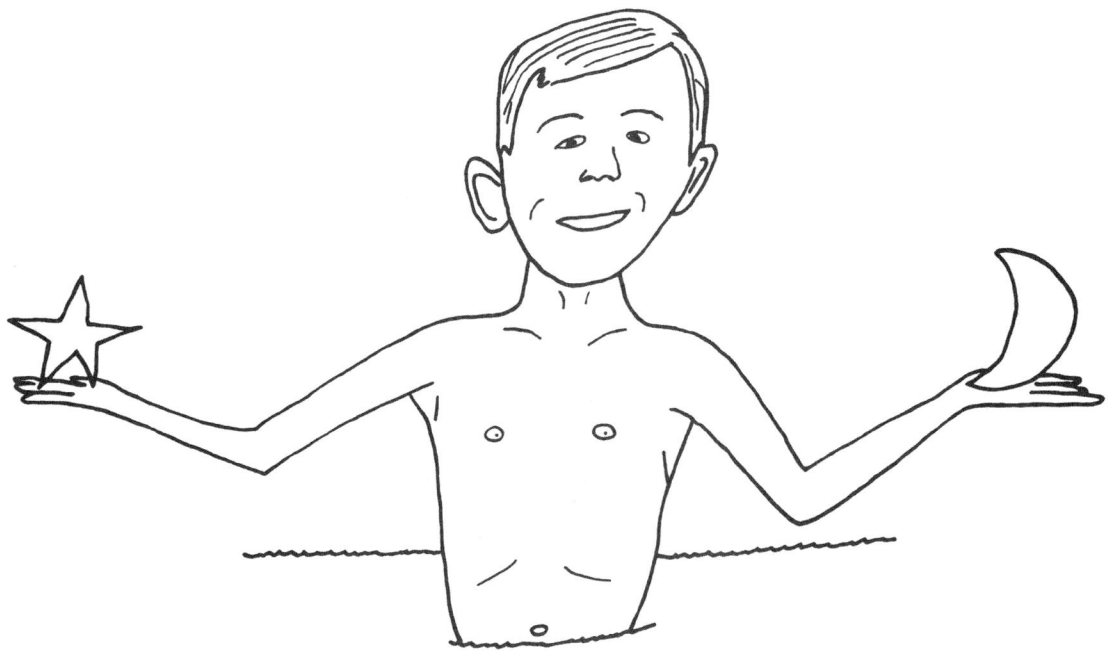

ELBOWS AND KNEES

I have a pair each of elbows and knees
That help me to balance and stand as I please.
There's a part of my mind that helps them adjust.
It's not as much thinking as learning to trust.
And so I can walk. I can run and I play.
With my knees and my elbows I'm finding my way.

They're not very pretty.
(I scrape them a lot.)
But I've come to accept
They're the best that I've got.

And I wonder if also there is deep in my mind
Something that helps me when I'm caught in a bind.

Determination and courage

For me are those keys
That keep me in balance like elbows and knees.
A gift and a choice, they're a part of me, too.
In difficult times they help me get through.
And though I can't see them like elbows and knees

There is nothing more vital
In life than are these.

GOLDILOCKS FROG

Goldie Frog broke protocol and took a brazen dare,
Waited 'til the bears left home and ate some porridge there.
When the bears returned they said they'd call the cops
But Goldie Frog said she'd heat some more to make them lick their chops.
"Not too hot!" said Poppa Bear. "The stuff will burn my lip."
But Goldie Frog just laughed when he spat out his first sip.
"I can cool mine down," she said, "with a little puff of air,
Something you can't do 'cause you're just a stupid bear!"
Her counsel that the bears should wait and let the porridge thicken
Abruptly ended with the words, "Mmmmm! Tastes like chicken!"

Goldie Frog! Oh, Goldie Frog!
The porridge was too hot
But lucky for the bears,

THE REST OF YOU WAS NOT!

EATING OKRA

Blackened, grilled,
Sauteed real hot,
Boiled for hours –
Looks like snot!
Nothing seems
To hide the taste!
Grocery dollars
Gone to waste!
Over roaring campfires
Hanging on a stick,
Okra never fails!
It always
Makes me sick!
"Hide the taste!" I thought
And had it batter fried.
There's not a single thing
That I haven't tried.
I went to ask my Grandma
Just the other day,
"How should you eat okra?"
There had to be a way.
She looked through all her cookbooks
Trying to recall
But I liked Grandpa's answer:

"JUST ONE WAY. THAT'S NOT AT ALL!:

BUTTONS FROM THE SKY

In the closet depths I found my favorite suit
And a nice silk shirt! A leather belt to boot.
I was going on a business trip and packed them all away
And saved them for a meeting with my boss today.
I tried it on this morning. It had a tighter fit
And I had to be real careful when it was time to sit.
My boss gave us a speech. It was his best, I think,
But as dinner settled in my suit began to shrink.
It was not the words but the suit that made me cry
And I think it was the sobbing that brought the buttons from the sky.
And with the raining buttons laughter also fell
And the story is a favorite my office likes to tell.
And if there is a moral to this sad, sad tale of woe
It's to try on all your traveling clothes just before you go.

This poem was written on the set of the George Clooney movie, **Up in the Air.** I was an extra. My suit was too tight!

LEMONADE

Lemonade
in the shade
with the summer breezes blowing.
Nice and cool,
A swimming pool
Down my throat now flowing.
Summertime
I think that I'm
Getting hot again.
In fact I figure
If my glass were bigger
I'd be jumping in!

MUDDY SHOES

Muddy shoes are bad, I know,
Evidence of melting snow
And yet the little one who trods
Calculates not the odds
Of judgment from a steely frown
As he ambles hallways down
To wake his mother with a kiss
And share with her a secret, this:
A flower from the garden grown,
The seeds of spring finally shown,
And joy enough in such great news
To surely pardon muddy shoes.

SOGGY BUNS

I went into a restaurant
To have a simple meal
Surprised to find inside my box
Something awful to reveal.
No, it wasn't something living
Or thin catsup as it runs
But the worst of all encounters:
Hamburgers with soggy buns!
I couldn't even pick it up
Without my hand becoming wet
And when I told the manager
He said something I'll ne'er forget.
"Sir, we carefully craft each meal.
We're well aware of what's inside!
We've always had these soggy buns
And we serve each one with pride!
I have soggy buns
Each and every place I go.
I like my soggy buns
And so does everyone I know!"
I was completely speechless
And did not know what to do
For I like my buns firm and dry
And I think my wife does too!

THE FALLEN WAVE

Towering it loomed, cresting towards the sun.
Foaming! Falling forcefully towards the sand, then done.
Lapping – oh so quietly – at castles made of sand
Seems a bitter ending for a wave that stood so grand.
And yet the water rushes back to build another giant
For the ocean does not long remain docile and compliant.
The fallen wave has life again, is constantly renewed
As are youthful dreams that failure once subdued.
There is a tempest brewing far, far out at sea
And dreams that are much stronger that yet give life to me.

There is rises! Now it falls.
Yet ever, always, my dream calls.

THE NINTH PIG

She started out behind,
The smallest of the litter.
It would have been quite easy
To grow up mad and bitter.
But she never gave up trying
And always found a way
And the ninth pig of the litter
Has won first prize today.
Something happens deep inside
When someone does their best
As though through disadvantage
We are sometimes blessed.
No one can imagine
How someone else may grow
In the daily turbulence
Of mortal to and fro.
It took the smallest pig
To help me realize
That success does not depend alone
On brawn or brains or size.
It depends on attitude
That just will not give in
To overcome the obstacles
And have a chance to win.

ESCUCHEN!

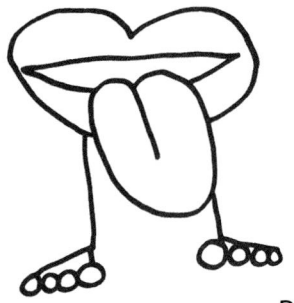

According to my Spanish class
Which I was fortunate to pass
"Escuchen" means to listen well
But there was about a ten year spell
Beginning in my middle teens
When I had not tendency nor means
To "escuchen" much in any tongue,
Indeed to use both lip and lung
To persuade folks to my point of view
As no one knew the things I knew.
And though people sometimes say I've changed
It's really just how I've arranged
My words in rhythm and in rhyme.
I'm still the same for all this time!
For I believe that good will win,
That when you fail to try again,
That love's the world's most potent force
And honesty's the clearest course,
That faith and hope and deepest trust
In the end will win and must
And though my voice is softer now
And there are wrinkles in my brow
The conviction that a young man held
Holds as firm as any weld.
For all the trials I've ever known
My certainty has only grown
So call me stubborn if you will:
This is what I stand for still.

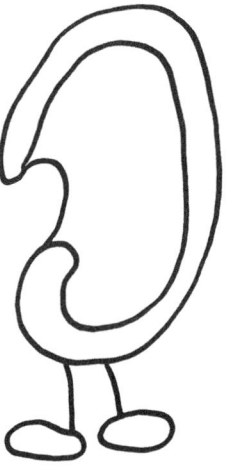

ONE TOO MANY

We went out to the county fair to see a man called "Snake"
Who let those serpents climb on him for hours with no break.
I did my best to count them. It was a hundred, pretty nigh,
But Mr. Snake complained, "There's something gone awry!
We'd better get to looking 'cause I think that one is missing!"
And suddenly my mother's purse moved and started hissing!
She screamed and threw it up and it opened in the air
And the snake that slithered out landed in her hair!
There are certain pitches that humans cannot hear
And I'm lucky that I only lost the hearing in one ear.
If they were keeping records how far a snake was hurled
I think my mother would be known as champion of the world!
But she's not one to brag. She won't talk about it any
Except to say that as for snakes,

"ONE IS ONE TOO MANY!"

THE COMMON TRIBULATIONS

We are not above
the common tribulations
that confront, confuse
and trouble our relations.
Often it's the little things
that start with just a trickle
yet add up to remind us
how life can be so fickle.
High atop the mountain
and in the moment next
frustrated, angry
and, most of all, perplexed
at how the tumble happened
– Oh! – so very quickly
and life that seemed so smooth
has somehow gotten prickly.
For no matter how you think
life has made you wise
the common tribulations
will catch you by surprise.
And then it's time to take
a step back from the fray,
reflect and reevaluate
and go about your day
and hopefully take with you
a whole new set of mind
that leaves your tribulations
and troubles far behind.

AN ACT OF TRUE KINDNESS

An act of true kindness
Is an incredible sight
For taking the wrong
And making it right.
Give someone who's hungry
A piece of your bread
And you'll find that your spirit
Also is fed.
Give someone who's weak
A strong hand to hold
And look for the same
Should you dare to grow old.
Some people need time.
Try spending a while
Sharing a story,
A laugh or a smile.

Kindness is never
One way like a street.
Without it no person
Is ever complete.
Isn't there someone
You can help out today?
If you think just a moment
You might find a way.
Reach out with your thoughts,
Your heart and your mind
To try to bring forward
Those left far behind.
Try it today
As never before
Then go out tomorrow
And do even more.

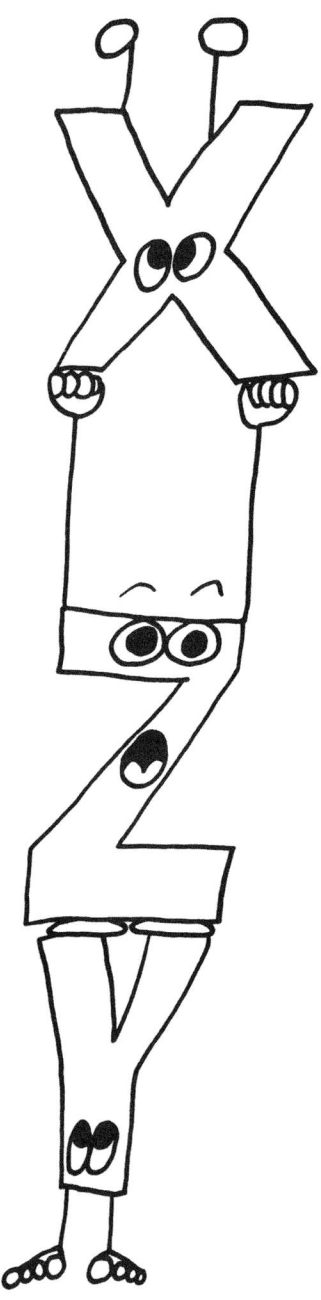

X AND Y AND Z

I wonder what the reason is
For X and Y and Z.
Do we really need them?
It's not so clear to me.
X could be replaced
By C and K and S.
We might be better off
If we had one letter less.
Now Y is simply silly,
Both consonant and vowel!
Why the newest of our readers
Might just throw in the towel!
Z has no defenders
Except the chimpanzee
So let's call it something else!
That would be fine with me.
Ecksept I am not sure
How this looks to ewe.
Without these letters I'm afraid
Life might be, well, a zoo!
Not everything is logical
And it's a good thing that it's not
So let's keep X and Y and Z
'Cause I like them a lot!

SNAKE SKINS AND LOCUST SHELLS

Reminders that they once were little
There they lie, broken and brittle.
Once a shelter lived inside
The living part has split it wide.
In its new skin the snake has grown
And slithered off to parts unknown.
The locust grew and left as well
And what remains is just this shell.
That seems to be the way life goes.
Something's lost as something grows.
The locust and the snake have gone
And as I grow, I too, move on.

THE SQUIRRELS' QUARREL

The squirrels quarrel
Over acorns in the fall
As if a single squirrel
Could store and eat them all.
The squirrels quarrel with the birds
When spring comes into season
But why I cannot tell!
They don't seem to need a reason.
The squirrels quarrel all day long
And it makes me laugh a lot
'Cause I like to think I'm different
But you know - I'm really not!

GLUE

Helps to make a picture,
Holds puzzles in their place.
Sticks two things together,
Puts stars upon your face.
Be loyal to your friends
And always say what's true.
Do the right thing every day
And you won't be needing glue.

THE PAINTER AND THE POET

The poet sees the painter
correcting his mistakes,
who makes the painting beautiful
in spite of all he makes,
for the painter paints them over
to make his picture true
while the poet points them out
and for that same reason, too.

UNCLE ALFRED'S EARS

My Uncle Alfred was very strange.
Of that, there is no doubt.
He could raise his eyebrows one at a time
And wiggle his ears all about.
People came from miles around
When Alfred was just a mere lad
And told his parents how lucky they were
And what a talent he had.
Uncle Alfred took it all in,
The spotlight, glory and fame,
And though he was never quite normal
He was able his pride to keep tame.
"I never did nothing to earn it,"
He told me one day on his stoop,
"For talent is kind of like ice cream.
It's good! Every flavor your scoop.
Yours might be vanilla or chocolate.
I might prefer peppermint.
Use all your talents for good
And enjoy them for they're heaven sent!"
With that he wiggled his ears
And gave me a wink and a nod
And I think of him often and well
Even though he was, frankly, quite odd.

CAMP CURE

I just found a tick on my pants.
The lunch that I brought is covered with ants.
Chiggers and fleas are making me scratch
And my ankles are red like an apple or match.
Spiders and bedbugs live in my sheet!
Camp is where nature - those bugs! - and I meet.
So I twitch through the night and rise with the dawn.
The bugs seem to like the sprays I put on.
I got bit by a snake and finned by a fish.
I asked to go camping and I got my wish.
I spent thirteen days in a bunk with a mouse
But tomorrow camp's over! I'll be back at the house.
It's been nigh a month since I've had a shower
So let's hope there's hot water enough for an hour.
For I've fought and I've battled and, yes, I've endured
But as for this camping

Don't worry!

I'm cured!

SLOW NOTION

I lie upon the beach
Free from any motion
Listening to the seagulls
Fly above the ocean.
And as I start to rise
I get a sudden notion:
Before I went to sleep
I should have used the lotion!

MY TEACHER IS...

My teacher is a treasure.
My teacher is a saint.
My teacher's glad it's three o'clock
'Cause what she is...

My teacher knows her science.
She knows her 'rithmatic.
She knows when she has had enough,
That's why she...

My teacher loves her students.
My teacher loves this class.
My teacher says she'll go insane
If all of us...

My teacher said she'd miss us.
She said, "Most terribly!"
My teacher got committed
And they threw away...

My teacher knew my name.
My teacher knew my face.
My principal said that when he asked
No one would...

I'm searching on the internet
To find some way to reach her
Can she talk me out of it?
I want to...

...A TREASURE

...we ain't!

...called in sick!

...don't pass!

...the key!

...take her place!

...be a teacher!

THESE GEESE DON'T FLY ON TUESDAYS

The sun was setting that Tuesday eve
As I neared the mountain top
But even with my lack of time
The scene before me made me stop.
A giant waterfall
Was dammed completely dry.
Geese that should be heading south
Wouldn't flap their wings to fly.
The trail that led to the highest peak
Was blocked by a giant gate.
A sign on the nearby cabin said,
"He who knocks, must wait."
"Hello," I called, "What's happened here?"
"Is everything okay?"
I never saw the man inside
But here's what I heard him say:
"These geese don't fly on Tuesdays!
The fish don't swim after eight.
We never take a chance here!
If we do, we're always late.
The waterfall doesn't run in summer.
We don't harvest grain in fall,
And if we do not water them,
These trees don't grow at all.

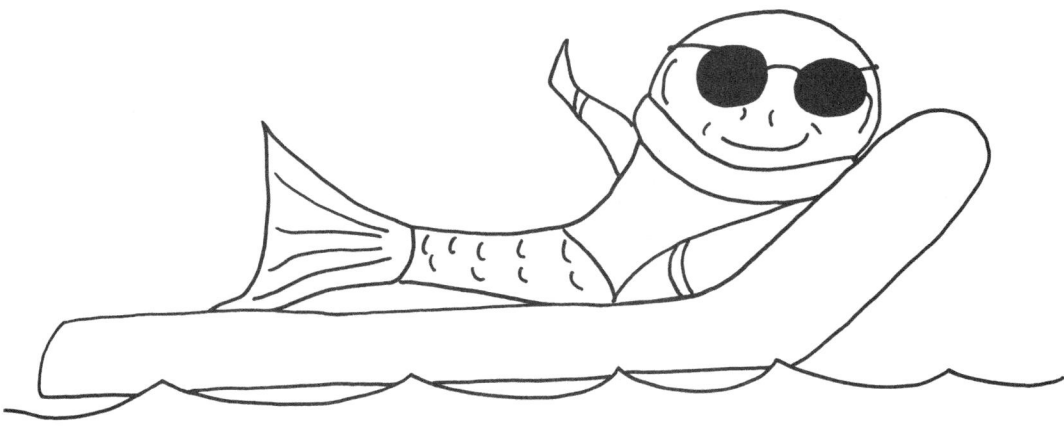

We don't have leaves to rake!
We never have grass to mow.
There's nothing that we want to learn!
We know all there is to know.
I won't climb that mountain
And I won't take that trail.
I won't try a thing that's new!
That way I'll never fail."

The woods were strangely silent
And the air was dead to sound.
The flowers that once had bloomed here
Returned to barren ground.
The best thing I could do
Was to leave that man in peace,
But I threw a rock as I climbed the trail
And off flew all the geese.

THE FATTED CALF

I went to hunt the buffalo
Across the fruited plains
So you would not have to eat
Refrigerate remains.
I saw many buffalo,
A thousand maybe more,
But I couldn't figure out
What this bow and arrow's for!
I stalked rabbits and beavers and ground hogs,
Squirrels, dove, and deer,
But my hunting skills have failed me!
I have none, I fear.
I'm afraid that I may never
Slay the fatted calf
But I brought home a pizza
And you can have a half.

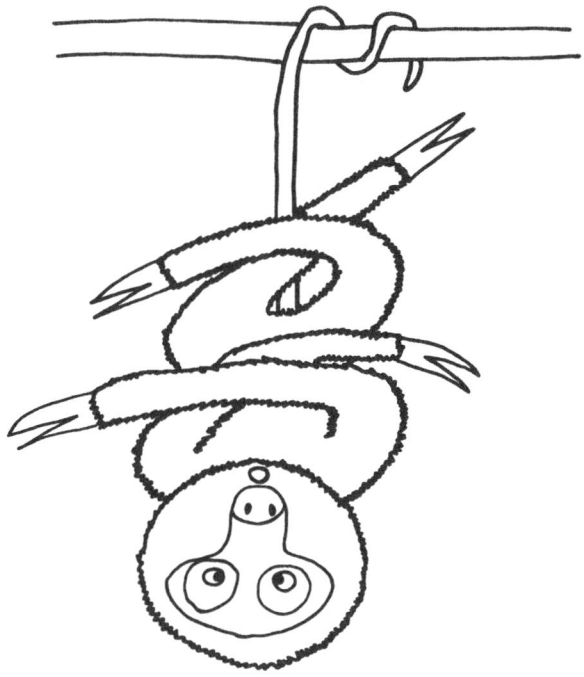

THE MUTANT TWO-TOED SLOTH LEARNS TO COUNT

One was easy, so was two.
Each toe he had gave him a clue.
A paw was free, then he counted to three.
With five toes and a tail he clung to the tree.
His head hung down when he counted to four
But with toed back feet he could do more.
On one of them he counted five and six!
He impressed his friends with mathematical tricks.
In the back of his mind a voice said, "Wait!"
But he bravely went on to seven and eight.
Survival instincts did not yet fail.
From the highest limb he still hung by his tail.
If he'd have stopped there he would have been fine
But the two-toed sloth counted to nine.

MY CELL PHONE

It rings me in the car.
It rings in sun or rain.
It really is convenient,
But today it is a pain!
Every time I get away
My cell phone rings to spoil it.
Even in the bathroom!
And now, deep in the toilet.

The drawing is dated. Sadly, the experience is not.

NAMING THE RABBITS

Twenty-two rabbits with cottontail rears,
Eighty-eight paws and forty-four ears!
The children can call each rabbit by name
But to my adult eyes they all look the same.
It's a matter of time I guess and suppose
To find something special in the touch of a nose,
The blink of an eye or the turn of a head.
There are too many things I'm watching instead
Like deadlines and schedules and bills overdue,
Things that a child called me never knew.
And thinking of this I realize again
That life can be simple for me like back then.
But slowing down life takes changing some habits
So I'm watching the children and naming the rabbits.

THE BEST AT STINKY

I chased a skunk into the woods
and much to my dismay
it welcomed me not with a kiss
but instead its awful spray!
I know not why it felt a call
to have such a bad reaction.
For fourteen days I have bathed
yet still reek its olfaction!
Tomato juice don't cut it!
Don't think I didn't try.
They tell me I'd smell better
if I'd just up and die!
But I think I've learned a lesson
that I'll pass on to you:
There are some things in this life
It's better not to do.
Don't sniff your brother's shoes!
Don't pull your grandpa's pinky!
And don't mess around with skunks
'cause they're the best at stinky!

GOING TO THE DENTIST

I'm going to the dentist!
She's going to scratch and scrape.
I would do most anything
If I could just escape!
But then I think about
The time my tooth was throbbing.
"Take me to the dentist!"
I remember sobbing.
So here's a bit of wisdom
I almost forgot:
What's worse than going to the dentist?
Just one thing – that's not.

THE TRAMPOLINE OF LIFE

Up and down and on and off
The backyard trampoline
And I wonder, if I think a bit,
There's a lesson I can glean.
The children bounce each other.
Everyone's affected,
And in the life we lead today
We are "interconnected."
It's funny how the trampoline
Seems to bring two kids together.
Is love merely a happenstance
Or a kind of magic tether?
Some are flipping, shouting out.
Others, silent, sit.
Does what you get in life
Come from what's put into it?
There's a time for action
And there's a time for rest.
You'll need a bit of both
If you're to do your best.

There's bumping with the jumping.
Expect a knock or two!
Playing on the trampoline
Is still so fun to do!
And when someone is called home
It changes how I play.
I'm sad they had to go
But I jump on anyway!
For now it is my turn
To stretch out to the sky,
And on the trampoline of life
I'll be bouncing high!

From watching the children play on the trampoline with their cousin, Karen.

THE RAIN DANCE

They danced all day and through the night
In hopes the clouds would grow and might
Break the drought that for so long had cursed their native land
Never giving up through they could barely stand.
They kept their frantic pace through evening number seven
When the distant thunder announced a gift from heaven.
With energy renewed they left it not to chance
And everyone rushed out to celebrate in dance.
It rained three days and nights and all the lakes were filled
And everyone who danced that day had this thought instilled:

Faith must be persistent to show the greatest gains
And a rain dance only works when you dance until it rains.

FREE BALLOONS

I'm giving away free balloons,
Big and fat and round,
Hoping if you take one
My feet will reach the ground!

FREE BALLOONS

I gave away my free balloons
And now I haven't any.
It seems I've found the one thing worse
Than having one too many!

STARS TO CHASE

I woke up this morning
Lost in outer space
And everything I ever knew
Was gone without a trace.
What to do? I did not know
For all was new to me,
And I remember thinking
What a strange place this was to be.
But I shook the twinkle off a star,
Caught a comet by the tail,
Stretched the rings of Saturn
And used them as a sail.

And even though there is no wind
In outer space to blow
Imagination took me everywhere
I could ever want to go.
I didn't need a ticket
To buy myself a ride
For the greatest of adventures
Is what goes on inside.
There are no limits in my mind
Or in yours either, friend,
So think those thoughts you're thinking
When you have some time to spend.
And if you should ever catch me
In my old familiar place
Remember that, inside my head,
I've still got stars to chase!

"Stars to Chase" is the title poem for my book of the same name. About half of the poems in this book are from that one.

Alphabetical List of Poems

A Bucket of Sand	56
A Different Path	65
A Whole New Turn	100
Advice from my Aunt Winnie	113
All the Tea in China	102
An Act of True Kindness	133
An Apology to Camels	50
Arnot and Artu, the Llamas from France	11
As Is	110
Blinders on Horses	112
Butterfly Wings	89
Buttons from the Sky	124
Camp Cure	140
Chase it like a Seagull	63
Climb the Red Mountain	30
Clutter	71
Cookies by a Zombie	87
Courage is its own Reward	92
Determination Deep	119
Eating Okra	123
Eighteen Doctors	111
Elbows and Knees	121
Endgame	31
Escuchen	130
Fiddle-dee-do	55
Free Balloons	155
Glue	137
Going to the Dentist	151
Goldilocks Frog	122
I Don't Like Coffee	79
Invasion of the Woodpeckers	21
It's too Small	85
Ivan the Terrier	32
Ivan the Terrier's Tail	33
Juan Pablo Madrid	76
King Louie's Horse's Butt: a love story	40
Knocking on Pipes	49
Last Chance for the Big Purple Dog	60
Leading the Unicorn	54
Leap from your Dreams	18
Lemonade	125
Light Blue Alpacas	107
May Your Lips Always Be Long Enough	91
Muddy Shoes	126
My Butler	96
My Cell Phone	148

My Teacher is a Treasure	142
My Teacher's Underpants	94
Naming the Rabbits	149
Neanderthal Ned	97
Neanderthal Nell	Back Cover
No TV	70
Not Shakespeare	66
Of Colander's and Calendars	101
Old Cheese	72
Old School	104
Ollie the Bobble Head Boy	24
One Too Many	131
Our Eagle	83
Over and Over	108
Pause to Dream	64
Pinching the Dinosaur	75
Prophet the Llama	17
Puddles	3
Rain on Canvas	59
Roses	48
Sandals	57
Seagull for a Day	105
Shakespeare Frog	68
Share a Dream	103
Sharks to Chase	82
Slow Notion	141
Snake Skins and Locust Shells	135
Soggy Buns	127
Spirit and Memory	106
Spot, the Talking Bug	95
Standing on Boxes	88
Stars to Chase	156
Stubbing my Toe	62
Stubble	58
Super-Frog	12
Thank You, Candle Charm!	98
The Algebra Poem	80
The Ballad of Peanut Butter Pete	14
The Bed Sheet Parachute	4
The Best at Stinky	150
The Breath Holding Contest	38
The Common Tribulations	132
The Dead Snake's Bite	36
The Earthworms	46
The Fallen Wave	128
The Fatted Calf	146
The First Day Back	78
The Flatulent Flutist	44

The Little Pyromaniac	22
The Mutant Two-Toed Sloth Learns to Count	147
The Ninth Pig	129
The Otter Oughter	10
The Painter and the Poet	138
The Paths Divide	52
The Pig and the Poodle	74
The Pig has Wings	77
The Poet Laureate of Byrnes Mill	99
The Pythagorean Poem	81
The Rain Dance	154
The Squirrels' Quarrel	136
The Talking Feet	73
The Trampoline of Life	152
There's an Outhouse in Byrnes Mill	116
Therein was the Dawn	84
These Geese Don't Fly on Tuesdays	144
Thinking Upside Down	6
Too Much to Handle	109
Treed off	34
Turnabout Mountain	28
Two More Fiddles	114
Uncle Alfred's Ears	139
Walter Wupperman's Wings	26
Warrior in the Land of Kings	90
When the last Cloud's Past	120
Why Phyllis Burned the Barn	86
Wobbling Willie Woodard	118
X and Y and Z	134